Volume VIII
Report No. 84
May, 1973

The Joys and Sorrows Of Parenthood

Formulated by the
Committee on Public Education

Group for the Advancement of Psychiatry

Additional copies of this GAP Publication No. 84 are available at the following prices: 1-9, $4.00 each; 10-24 copies, list less 15 per cent; 25-99 copies, list less 20 per cent; 100-499 copies, list less 30 per cent.

Upon request the Publications Office of the Group for the Advancement of Psychiatry will provide a complete listing of GAP titles currently in print, quantity prices, and information on subscriptions assuring the receipt of new publications as they are released.

Orders amounting to less than $5.00 must be accompanied by remittance. All prices are subject to change without notice.

Please send your order and remittance to: Publications Office, Group for the Advancement of Psychiatry, 419 Park Avenue South, New York, New York 10016.

Standard Book Number 87318-117-4
Library of Congress Catalog Card Number 62-2872
Printed in the United States of America

TABLE OF CONTENTS

4 DISCIPLINE: SELF AND IMPOSED

5 VARIETIES OF PARENTHOOD EXPERIENCES

6 THE MIDDLE YEARS OF PARENTHOOD

This is the fourth in a series of publications comprising Volume VIII. For a list of other GAP publications on topics related to this subject, please see page 334.

STATEMENT OF PURPOSE

THE GROUP FOR THE ADVANCEMENT OF PSYCHIATRY has a membership of approximately 300 psychiatrists, most of whom are organized in the form of a number of working committees. These committees direct their efforts toward the study of various aspects of psychiatry and the application of this knowledge to the fields of mental health and human relations.

Collaboration with specialists in other disciplines has been and is one of GAP's working principles. Since the formation of GAP in 1946 its members have worked closely with such other specialists as anthropologists, biologists, economists, statisticians, educators, lawyers, nurses, psychologists, sociologists, social workers, and experts in mass communication, philosophy, and semantics. GAP envisages a continuing program of work according to the following aims:

1. To collect and appraise significant data in the field of psychiatry, mental health, and human relations;
2. To reevaluate old concepts and to develop and test new ones;
3. To apply the knowledge thus obtained for the promotion of mental health and good human relations.

GAP is an independent group, and its reports represent the composite findings and opinions of its members only, guided by its many consultants.

THE JOYS AND SORROWS OF PARENTHOOD *was formulated by the Committee on Public Education, which acknowledges on page 207 the participation of various committee members and GAP Fellows in the preparation of this report. The current members of this committee as well as all other committees and the officers of GAP as of April 1, 1973 are listed below.*

Julius Schreiber, Washington, D.C.
Robert H. Sharpley, Brookline, Mass.
Robert A. Solow, Beverly Hills
Kent A. Zimmerman, Berkeley

COMMITTEE ON ADOLESCENCE
Joseph D. Noshpitz, Washington, Chr.
Warren J. Gadpaille, Engelwood, Colo.
Charles A. Malone, Philadelphia
Silvio J. Onesti, Jr., Boston
Jeanne Spurlock, Nashville
Sidney L. Werkman, Denver

COMMITTEE ON AGING
Robert N. Butler, Washington, Chr.
Charles M. Gaitz, Houston
Alvin I. Goldfarb, New York
Lawrence F. Greenleigh, Los Angeles
Maurice E. Linden, Philadelphia
Prescott W. Thompson, San Jose, Calif.
Montague Ullman, Brooklyn
Jack Weinberg, Chicago

COMMITTEE ON CHILD PSYCHIATRY
Joseph M. Green, Tucson, Ariz., Chr.
E. James Anthony, St. Louis
James M. Bell, Canaan, N.Y.
Harlow Donald Dunton, New York
John F. Kenward, Chicago
John F. McDermott, Jr., Honolulu
Exie E. Welsch, New York
Virginia N. Wilking, New York

COMMITTEE ON THE COLLEGE STUDENT
Robert L. Arnstein, New Haven, Chr.
Harrison P. Eddy, New York
Malkah Tolpin Notman, Brookline, Mass.
Gloria C. Onque, Pittsburgh
Kent E. Robinson, Towson, Md.
Earle Silber, Chevy Chase, Md.
Tom G. Stauffer, White Plains, N.Y.

COMMITTEE ON THE FAMILY
Joseph Satten, San Francisco, Chr.
C. Christian Beels, Bronx, N.Y.
Ivan Boszormenyi-Nagy, Philadelphia
Murray Bowen, Chevy Chase
Henry U. Grunebaum, Boston
Margaret M. Lawrence, Pomona, N.Y.
Henry D. Lederer, Washington, D.C.
David Mendell, Houston
Norman L. Paul, Cambridge
Israel Zwerling, Bronx, N.Y.

COMMITTEE ON GOVERNMENTAL AGENCIES
Paul Chodoff, Washington, D.C., Chr.
William S. Allerton, Richmond
Albert M. Biele, Philadelphia
Sidney S. Goldensohn, New York
John E. Nardini, Washington, D.C.
Donald B. Peterson, Fulton, Mo.
Harvey L. P. Resnik, Chevy Chase, Md.
Harold Rosen, Baltimore

COMMITTEE ON INTERNATIONAL RELATIONS
Bryant M. Wedge, Washington, D.C., Chr.
Francis F. Barnes, Chevy Chase
Eric A. Baum, Cambridge
Eugene B. Brody, Baltimore
Alexander Gralnick, Port Chester, N.Y.
Rita R. Rogers, Torrance, Calif.
Bertram H. Schaffner, New York
Mottram P. Torre, New Orleans
Ronald M. Wintrob, Hartford

COMMITTEE ON MEDICAL EDUCATION
David R. Hawkins, Charlottesville, Chr.
Robert S. Daniels, Cincinnati
Raymond Feldman, Boulder, Colo.
Saul I. Harrison, Ann Arbor
Harold I. Lief, Philadelphia
John E. Mack, Boston
William L. Peltz, Longview, Vt.
David S. Sanders, Los Angeles
Robert A. Senescu, Albuquerque, N.M.
Roy M. Whitman, Cincinnati

COMMITTEE ON MENTAL HEALTH SERVICES
Merrill T. Eaton, Omaha, Chr.
Allan Beigel, Tucson, Ariz.
H. Keith H. Brodie, Menlo Park, Calif.
Eugene M. Caffey, Jr., Washington, D.C.
Archie R. Foley, New York
James B. Funkhouser, Richmond, Va.
Robert S. Garber, Belle Mead, N.J.
Stanley Hammons, Frankfort, Ky.
Alan I. Levenson, Tucson, Ariz.
W. Walter Menninger, Topeka
Donald Scherl, Boston
Perry C. Talkington, Dallas
Jack A. Wolford, Pittsburgh

COMMITTEE ON MENTAL RETARDATION
Henry H. Work, Washington, D.C., Chr.
Howard V. Bair, Parsons, Kans.
Stuart M. Finch, Ann Arbor
Leo Madow, Philadelphia
George Tarjan, Los Angeles
Warren T. Vaughan, Jr., Burlingame, Calif.
Thomas G. Webster, Washington, D.C.

COMMITTEE ON PREVENTIVE PSYCHIATRY
Stephen Fleck, New Haven, Chr.
Frederick Gottlieb, Sherman Oaks, Calif.
Benjamin Jeffries, Harper Woods, Mich.
Ruth W. Lidz, Woodbridge, Conn.
E. James Lieberman, Washington, D.C.
Mary E. Mercer, Nyack, N.Y.
Harris B. Peck, Bronx, N.Y.
Marvin E. Perkins, White Plains, N.Y.

COMMITTEE ON PSYCHIATRY AND LAW
Carl P. Malmquist, Minneapolis, Chr.
Edward T. Auer, St. Louis
John Donnelly, Hartford
Peter B. Hoffman, Charlottesville, Va.
A. Louis McGarry, Brookline, Mass.
Seymour Pollack, Los Angeles
Alan A. Stone, Cambridge
Gene L. Usdin, New Orleans

COMMITTEE ON PSYCHIATRY AND RELIGION
Sidney S. Furst, New York, Chr.
Stanley A. Leavy, New Haven
Richard C. Lewis, New Haven
Earl A. Loomis, Jr., New York
Albert J. Lubin, Woodside, Calif.
Mortimer Ostow, New York
Bernard L. Pacella, New York
Michael R. Zales, Greenwich, Conn.

COMMITTEE ON PSYCHIATRY AND SOCIAL WORK
John A. MacLeod, Cincinnati, Chr.
C. Knight Aldrich, Newark, N.J.
Maurice R. Friend, New York
Herbert C. Modlin, Topeka
John C. Nemiah, Boston
Alexander S. Rogawski, Los Angeles
Charles B. Wilkinson, Kansas City, Mo.

COMMITTEE ON PSYCHIATRY IN INDUSTRY
Clarence J. Rowe, St. Paul, Chr.
Spencer Bayles, Houston
Thomas L. Brannick, Imola, Calif.
Duane Q. Hagen, St. Louis
R. Edward Huffman, Asheville, N.C.
Herbert L. Klemme, Topeka
Alan A. McLean, New York
David E. Morrison, Topeka
John Wakefield, Cambridge

COMMITTEE ON PSYCHOPATHOLOGY
George E. Ruff, Philadelphia, Chr.
Wagner H. Bridger, New York
Sanford I. Cohen, Boston
Daniel X. Freedman, Chicago
Paul E. Huston, Iowa City
Jack H. Mendelson, Boston
Richard E. Renneker, Los Angeles
Charles Shagass, Philadelphia
Albert J. Silverman, Ann Arbor, Mich.
George E. Vaillant, Boston

COMMITTEE ON RESEARCH
Morris A. Lipton, Chapel Hill, Chr.
Stanley E. Eldred, Belmont, Mass.
Louis A. Gottschalk, Irvine, Calif.
Donald F. Klein, Glen Oaks, N.Y.
Gerald L. Klerman, Boston
Ralph R. Notman, Brookline, Mass.
Alfred H. Stanton, Belmont, Mass.
Eberhard H. Uhlenhuth, Chicago

COMMITTEE ON SOCIAL ISSUES
Roy W. Menninger, Topeka, Chr.
Viola W. Bernard, New York
Roderic Gorney, Los Angeles
Lester Grinspoon, Boston
Joel S. Handler, Evanston, Ill.
Judd Marmor, Los Angeles
Peter B. Neubauer, New York
Perry Ottenberg, Philadelphia
Kendon W. Smith, Piermont
Raymond G. Wilkerson, Chicago

COMMITTEE ON THERAPEUTIC CARE
Robert W. Gibson, Towson, Md., Chr.
Bernard Bandler, Boston
Ian L. W. Clancey, Ottawa
Thomas E. Curtis, Chapel Hill
Harold A. Greenberg, Bethesda
Milton Kramer, Cincinnati
Orlando B. Lightfoot, Boston
Melvin Sabshin, Chicago
Robert E. Switzer, Topeka

Committee on Therapy

Justin Simon, Berkeley, Chr.
Henry W. Brosin, Tucson, Ariz.
Peter H. Knapp, Boston
Eugene Meyer, Baltimore
William C. Offenkrantz, Chicago
Franz K. Reichsman, Brooklyn
Lewis L. Robbins, Glen Oaks, N.Y.
Richard I. Shader, Newton Center, Mass.
Harley C. Shands, New York
Herbert Weiner, Stanford, Calif.

Contributing Members

Marvin L. Adland, Chevy Chase
Carlos C. Alden, Jr., Buffalo
William H. Anderson, Lansing, Mich.
Charlotte G. Babcock, Pittsburgh
Grace Baker, New York
Walter E. Barton, Washington, D.C.
Anne R. Benjamin, Chicago
Ivan C. Berlien, Coral Gables, Fla.
Sidney Berman, Washington, D.C.
Grete L. Bibring, Cambridge
Edward G. Billings, Denver
Carl A. L. Binger, Cambridge
H. Waldo Bird, St. Louis
Wilfred Bloomberg, Boston
Peter W. Bowman, Pownal, Me.
Matthew Brody, Brooklyn
Ewald W. Busse, Durham
Dale C. Cameron, Geneva
Norman Cameron, Tucson, Ariz.
Gerald Caplan, Boston
Hugh T. Carmichael, Washington, D.C.
Jules V. Coleman, New Haven
Robert Coles, Cambridge
Harvey H. Corman, New York
Frank J. Curran, New York
William D. Davidson, Washington, D.C.
Leonard J. Duhl, Berkeley
Lloyd C. Elam, Nashville
Joel Elkes, Baltimore
Joseph T. English, New York
Louis C. English, Pomona, N.Y.
O. Spurgeon English, Narberth, Pa.
Jack R. Ewalt, Boston
Dana L. Farnsworth, Boston
Malcolm J. Farrell, Waverley, Mass.
Alfred Flarsheim, Chicago
Alan Frank, Albuquerque, N.M.
Lawrence Z. Freedman, Chicago
Moses M. Frohlich, Ann Arbor
Daniel H. Funkenstein, Boston
Albert J. Glass, Chicago
Milton Greenblatt, Boston
Maurice H. Greenhill, Scarsdale, N.Y.
John H. Greist, Indianapolis
Roy R. Grinker, Sr., Chicago
Ernest M. Gruenberg, Poughkeepsie, N.Y.
Joel S. Handler, Evanston, Ill.
Edward O. Harper, Cleveland, Ohio
Mary O'Neill Hawkins, New York
J. Cotter Hirschberg, Topeka
Edward J. Hornick, New York
Joseph Hughes, Philadelphia
Portia Bell Hume, Berkeley
Irene M. Josselyn, Phoenix
Jay Katz, New Haven
Sheppard G. Kellam, Chicago
Marion E. Kenworthy, New York
Ernest W. Klatte, Santa Ana, Calif.
Othilda M. Krug, Cincinnati
Zigmond M. Lebensohn, Washington
Robert L. Leopold, Philadelphia
David M. Levy, New York
Reginald S. Lourie, Washington, D.C.
Alfred O. Ludwig, Boston
Jeptha R. MacFarlane, Westbury, N.Y.
Sydney G. Margolin, Denver
Helen V. McLean, Chicago
Karl A. Menninger, Topeka
James G. Miller, Washington, D.C.
John A. P. Millet, New York
Kenneth J. Munden, Memphis
Lucy D. Ozarin, Bethesda, Md.
Rudolph G. Novick, Lincolnwood, Ill.
Irving Philips, San Francisco
Charles A. Pinderhughes, Boston
Vivian Rakoff, Toronto
Eveoleen N. Rexford, Cambridge
Milton Rosenbaum, Bronx, N.Y.
W. Donald Ross, Cincinnati
Lester H. Rudy, Chicago
Kurt O. Schlesinger, San Francisco
Elvin V. Semrad, Boston
Calvin F. Settlage, Sausalito, Calif.
Benson R. Snyder, Cambridge
John P. Spiegel, Waltham, Mass.
Brandt F. Steele, Denver
Eleanor A. Steele, Denver
Rutherford B. Stevens, New York
Graham C. Taylor, Montreal

COMMITTEE ACKNOWLEDGMENTS

The Committee on Public Education was under the chairmanship of Peter A. Martin, M.D., when this report was formulated.

At that time the committee also included the following members of GAP: Leo H. Bartemeier, Robert J. Campbell, Dana L. Farnsworth, Marion E. Kenworthy, James A. Knight, John P. Lambert, Norman L. Loux, Mildred R. Mitchell Bateman, Mabel Ross, Julius Schreiber, Robert H. Sharpley, Miles F. Shore, Robert A. Solow, and Kent A. Zimmerman.

Drs. Farnsworth and Kenworthy, both past presidents, of GAP, are now contributing rather than active members of the Group. The current chairman of its Committee on Public Education is Dr. Shore.

The committee wishes to express its appreciation to two GAP Fellows who aided in the formulation of this report: Drs. Jim Howard Earls and Michael MuCulloch.

INTRODUCTION

Target audiences and focus of report

In keeping with its primary function, the Committee on Public Education of the Group for the Advancement of Psychiatry prepared this report with the public in mind as its target audience. We hope it also will be a useful reference for high school and college courses in family living and of value to those professionals involved with the interests of the general non-professional reader.

The focus of the book is on parenthood as a stage in the life cycle of the individual. It presents parenthood as a period of life offering the opportunity for continuing personal growth and development. Though not often emphasized, the experience of one's emotional growth and maturation is one of the most important joys of parenthood and probably its most enduring one. It is an active joy, derived from doing and becoming as opposed to the passive joy of receiving. It is a product of successful completion of a stage of life leading to increased ease in functioning. Such joy is an indication of positive mental health. In this way, parenthood is more than a test of endurance at whose conclusion the saintly man may whisper, "And now, Oh Lord, may I go my way in peace?" To be prevented are the sorrow-filled experiences too often observed wherein the pitfalls of parenthood have ensnared the unprepared traveler.

A disclaimer: what the report is not

Among the strengths of the Group for the Advancement of Psychiatry is the circulation of committee reports through the entire membership; as a result, the end product is a Group report. From this procedure, we already know that to some readers this report will appear to be too general. It is not specific enough in detailing variations in the experience of parenthood among families of minority groups and of different ethnic, socioeconomic, and cultural backgrounds. The Committee on the Family has several publications dealing with the cultural group variations and different styles of family life for different ethnic, race, and social class groupings.[1] These reports emphasize that the family may not be identified as a structural unit without reference to the surrounding social system and that the responsibilities of parents toward their children may not be divorced from their other roles in the larger society. They illustrate the complexities created by many variances that we do not discuss in this book.

On the other hand, this report will be considered by others as too technical, too often using professional jargon and thereby limiting effective communication and public education. Mindful of the pitfalls at both ends of the communication spectrum, we have sought to strike a reasonable balance while leaning toward less complexity and less inclusiveness.

The composition of our committee spans the broad field of psychiatry. It ranges from the age groups of young residents in psychiatry (GAP Fellows) to old-timers with fifty years of experience, in varying clinical, administrative, and research areas. It includes the full gamut of religious and ethnic backgrounds. The only common denominator is that of middle-class background. This report represents private experiences and is thus not a scholarly research publication. We are aware that our observations have been culturally determined, and it might be inferred that the views on parenthood expressed in the report apply only to dominant middle-class family patterns. But we are not stressing parent roles or variations of parent roles. Many experiences are similar for all parents. Generally, the process of parenthood is not so different, having many aspects applicable across the board of various cultures. We are writing for many groups whose members can extract from this report what will be of value to them. Hopefully, the accumulation of experiences and literature will allow for the understanding of variations to be considered by our committee at another time.

To clarify our purpose further, it is important also to state what this report is not. It is not a how-to-do-it book. It is not a book offering methods of applying principles to problems presented to parents by children. It does not address itself to such questions as nudity in the family, or sleeping habits. It does not speak to such questions as these, which parents ask.

What the report is

This book applies itself to questions we think parents should ask themselves: What have I learned? How have I grown? What can I do now that I couldn't do before? What joys and pleasures am I experiencing in addition to enduring parenthood?

Many books have been written through the years in which parent-child relations, their consequences, and the processes involved have been viewed almost entirely from the bias of the parent's responsibility for the child. An overwhelming amount of material has been written about the stages of child development, the needs of children, and their care. In contrast, relatively little has been written about the thought processes of parents and about what it is to be a parent. This report suffers in spots from the child-emphasis style of thinking. Repeatedly we had to bring ourselves back to focus on the parent instead of the child.

The full development of the parent's personality through his successful experience as a parent allows him to move on to his post-parenthood life with a greater ability for fulfillment in other interpersonal relationships. Hopefully, the experience of parenthood will be relatively free of anxiety, guilt and depression. Hopefully, too, it will be an experience promoting mental health, with relatively easy separation at its termination for both parent and child and with easy movement into the next stage of their life cycles. The purpose of this book, then, is to promote mental health in parents through public education. Characteristic of the later years in life is a search for meaning. This report offers personal growth and development as giving an important meaning to life. It deals with expectations for oneself rather than for the children—the goals of a person apart from his children.

Reference

1. Group for the Advancement of Psychiatry, INTEGRATION AND CONFLICT IN FAMILY BEHAVIOR, GAP Report No. 27A (New York: The Group, 1968).

1

THE STAGES OF PARENTHOOD

The family is the psychological field of study

As we indicated in the Introduction, the Committee agreed that there was no reason for another book on children's needs and certainly not for still another book on how to rear children. Our purpose is to address ourselves to parents in such a way as to encourage them to think of parenthood as a creative experience in self-growth and not as an onerous guilt-laden duty that saddles them with full responsibility for any results that may prove less than ideal. Despite this emphasis, we often found our writing to be automatically child oriented. The welfare of the child continuously took preference over the well-being of the parent, and the chapters that follow still show evidence of this long-standing orientation.

Of course, focusing on parenthood itself has an artificial quality. The needs of the parent cannot be separated from the simultaneous needs of the child and the responsibilities of marriage. The total family, and not its individual members, is the psychological field of study. Ideally, the needs of the child, of the parent, and of the mate mutually reinforce one another. When this occurs, the joys of parenthood are experienced. Practically, however, these needs are to varying degrees in opposition to one another, imposing frustrations and sorrows and forcing mutual adaptation.

At various points, in order to describe them at all, we have had to deal with the activities of parenthood as though they were separate and isolated. This is not to deny the complexity of parent-child interactions and the many variables in such relationships. We wish to emphasize the mutuality of parent-child interactions, the mutual influence of developing parents on developing children. Often the literature appears to assume that the child, encountering his parents' attitudes as he grows and changes, interacts with a fixed quantity: the adult. Yet adulthood itself is a developmental process. Not only does the parent change under the impact of forces within him and outside him, but the outer influence of the child exerts special force on the adaptation and personality development of the father and mother.

Parenting involves reliving the parent's own childhood experiences during each stage through which the child passes.[1] Parents and children develop together and interact with each other.

Parenting offers an intense experience of feeling what another individual is feeling (empathy), thus enlarging the adult's capacity in this vital area of human relationship. The fuller development of the adult's personality through his successful parenting experiences allows him to move on to his post-parenting life with a greater ability for fulfillment in other interpersonal relations. Ideally, the parenting experience is relatively free of anxiety, guilt, and depression. Ideally, both parents and children grow through this stage with successful resolution of their deep-seated ties and move freely to the next stage of their life cycles. But we know that the ideal is never attained. This report speaks to the struggle that takes place within parents as they experience their parenthood.

Stage of parenthood—indefinite versus limited period

Therese Benedek defines parenthood as a psychobiological process that ends only with the death of the parent.[2] To expect its reciprocal psychobiological involvements to end with the maturation of the children is a fallacy probably based on the experience that children appear to outgrow their parents when they themselves become parents. It is from this stimulus that the new grandparents begin to relive the memories of past experiences; their parenthood is timeless. This is a most important understanding.

Life, however, is not a static process and an individual cannot forever remain a parent. It is not healthy for him or for the child. Timely resolution of the relationship with freedom for each is the goal.

The healthy resolution of the parent-child relationship was expressed by Kahlil Gibran with his poet's insight into human nature:

> Your children are not your children
> They are sons and daughters of Life's longing for itself.
> They come through you but not from you.
> And though they are with you yet they belong not to you.
> You may give them your love but not your thoughts,
> For they have their own thoughts.
> You may house their bodies but not their souls.
> For their souls dwell in the house of tomorrow, which you cannot visit, not even in your dreams.
> You may strive to be like them, but seek not to make them like you.
> For life goes not backward nor tarries with yesterday.
> You are the bows from which your children as living arrows are sent forth.
> The archer sees the mark upon the path of the infinite and He bends you with His might that His arrows may go swift and far.
> Let your bending in the archer's hand be for gladness.
> For even as He loves the arrow that flies, so He loves also the bow that is stable.[3]

This recognition of the essentiality of children and parents becoming separate individuals at the end of the parenthood stage will be emphasized throughout these chapters.

Needs of parents

Parents have personal needs that conflict with their need to be a parent. Yet they seem to be ignorant of their personal needs. One explanation is that the instinct to preserve the species is strong in all living creatures and often stronger than the need for self-preservation. The interests of the young are often felt as more important than those of the parent. Examples of this abound in the animal world. One well known is that of the salmon, who swim upstream to lay their eggs and afterwards die. Parents often feel their needs (physical or psychological) as being secondary to those of their children. Unlike their children, parents form part of the mainstream of life and find it difficult to be objective.

There are very strong cultural influences in American society that value the care of the young above the needs of adults. Adults are viewed as being ideal, as "rugged individualists" who do not have changing needs. Their behavior patterns are thought to be final, established, unchanging. Children and adolescents may go through a number of developmental stages, but once they reach adulthood many people think their development is finished. The adult is supposed to stay basically the same in his thinking, needs, and responses, at least until he reaches middle age and has to develop new directions. And by the time he reaches middle age his children are usually mature, so that he is no longer an active parent. These views are not accurate. Parenting does not end when children marry and establish their own homes. Psychologically, the stage of parenthood may never end.

But parents are not just "vehicles" for the care of children. They are people, and parenthood is one phase in their total development as human beings, a development that never stops but continues from birth to death. The stage of parenthood is an extremely important one, obviously, both for the children and for the parents. But parents are not the only influence on their children. Social institutions also shape the personality of the child. Nor can parents devote all their resources to rearing their children. Some of their inner resources must remain available for their own continuing development as adults.

Opposing parental attitudes

Some parents react negatively to the idea of not being *totally* responsible for the child's personality development. At first glance, this appears to be a strange reaction. Parents have been told for years that all their resources must be expended on the children and that they are to blame for anything and everything that goes wrong with the child (the apple doesn't fall far from the tree). You would think they would appreciate relief from guilt. But some do not want to be relieved of guilt if the price they pay is the loss of a sense of complete power and control over the child. If something goes wrong in the child's life, they prefer it to be totally their fault rather than partially the result of forces in the environment. If it is the forces in the environment that are determining, they feel weak and helpless. Even the idea that they did something wrong may feel better to them than the fear that "No matter what I do, I cannot change the direction of my child's life."

Other parents cannot bear to feel guilt. They prefer to emphasize the forces in the environment and thus absolve themselves of all responsibility. They feel that they cannot live up to the idealized image of parenthood, that the external forces operating on their children are too strong for them to counterbalance. They contribute to that segment of our society which is not child oriented. Though we wish to stress the needs of parents in this book, we are well aware of the traumas caused by attitudes of rejection toward children. In some segments of our society, children are being had at random. There is much evidence that they are not valued, that they are neglected and mistreated more often than they are brought up well.

When you examine these two points of view, you can see that the same thing has gone wrong in each case. Here parental concern is too much a personal anxiety about their own reputation and status as parents and not an effective concern for the healthy needs of their children or of themselves. The parent has very strong needs, but he is covering them up and denying them, and they evidence themselves in a distorted way in the life of the child. It would be much better for everyone—especially the child—if parental needs were understood and met in a healthy way. For one thing, it would help the parent to bring up his children without so much guilt and debilitating anxiety.

Development should be viewed from a broad perspective. The human personality does not stop suddenly at the end of adolescence and remain permanently fixed; it is constantly changing. The parent changes as he lives through critical life experiences and interacts with various people in his environment. He learns how to maintain an equilibrium by adapting to the forces that press on him from various directions at different times. Each new stage of his life requires another adjustment of his psychic forces and a further development of his personality.

The stages of parenthood

Prior to the development of effective contraceptive devices, the first pregnancy usually followed so quickly after marriage that the major transition point in a woman's life was marriage itself. Today, pregnancy is a more deliberate step, one that couples can and often do postpone until they feel ready for it economically, socially, and psychologically. Getting ready, however, is not always a simple or an easy matter. Education in American schools is notably deficient in subjects most relevant to successful family life: sex, home maintenance, child care, interpersonal relationships, understanding others. The parents' preparation during pregnancy is usually confined to reading, consultation with friends and parents, and discussion between husband and wife. Often the wife receives a great deal of support from the physician who is caring for her during pregnancy, but his role is limited because he is usually not the physician who will later care for the child and watch over his health and growth.

Many of the emotional aspects of parenthood are seen in miniature during pregnancy, the period of preparation for parenthood. In early pregnancy the mother's chief concerns are weight gain, vomiting, malaise, and possible loss of the baby—all fears relating to the new way in which her body is functioning. If, at the very beginning, she can accept the likelihood that her bodily growth and development will proceed naturally, she is less likely to be overwhelmed with concern over her child's growth. Some women "never felt better" than during pregnancy. Their physical health is good, their mental attitude is one of joyous anticipation. They feel fulfilled and never worry.

Later in pregnancy, if the mother-to-be worries, it is about whether or not her child will be perfect, whether she will lose her husband's love during the time she feels awkward and unattractive, whether she will be blamed for anything that goes wrong. Or she may revel in the attention and care she receives. The prospective father becomes more aware of his increased responsibilities and of the fact that his wife can no longer focus exclusively on him. He may experience a real loss of her interest as she becomes more involved with her body and the foetus.

The transition to parenthood is abrupt. One day husband and wife are alone; the next, there is the sudden imposition of round-the-clock care and responsibility for a totally dependent infant. The mother's deep psychological and physiological functions help her to act as a mother, but though she receives meaning and gratification from her intimate relation with the infant, her need for him is relative and not absolute. The baby, on the other hand, has an absolute need for his mother—or for somebody who will perform the same functions she does. She gives and gives to the child, but the child cannot give her everything *she* needs. The greater the degree to which sole responsibility for the newborn infant is placed on her, the greater her degree of social deprivation. Her husband, however, can do a great deal to help her care for the child and support her emotionally. Fathers provide much early care in numerous societies, and many now are doing so in our own country.

Do fathers also go through a new stage of development when a child is born? They do indeed. Fatherhood is a special manifestation of the individual's own growth. The individual, after having achieved maturity, surpasses the growth of his own body and becomes able to produce a new individual. This means that as he grows into maturity, he feels confident that his physical and emotional growth are complete enough for him to use them to create a new physical and psychological individual: his child.

The man's earliest security and orientation to his world were learned through experiences with his mother. These early experiences of the father parallel those of the mother, and they are the origin of fatherliness as well as of motherliness. The husband responds to his wife's needs and "mothers" her through her pregnancy. Soon after the birth of the child he develops a direct relationship with his offspring, enjoys the child's response to care, and feels pleased and fulfilled in being a good father.

It is difficult to adjust to being a parent, and some writers seem to be able to look at parenthood only as a disruptive, upsetting "crisis" in a family. Yet rearing children is one of the most normal things a mother and father can do. Let us see how people who become parents, rather than concentrating on the event as though it were an illness, adapt to their new role and use it as a tool for their own personal development.[4]

One useful way of looking at parenthood is to divide it into four stages: anticipatory, honeymoon, plateau, and disengagement.

1. Anticipatory stage. Some people have looked forward to parenthood from the time they were children. One of their first thoughts was, "Some day I will be a parent. . . . This is the way I would like to raise my children." When a man and a woman get married, they start to think about becoming parents, and when pregnancy occurs they give special thought to how they will rear their children and what parenthood will mean to them. A great deal is known about the physical needs of the mother and her developing foetus during this time, but the psychological necessities for good mental health are much less well understood.

2. Honeymoon stage. The baby has come. During the first weeks and months of marriage, the husband and wife have to learn to live closely with each other. Each adds a whole new dimension to the other's life. During the early months of parenthood, a great deal of interpersonal adjustment and learning takes place as the attachment between parent and child is formed and the members of the family learn new roles and relations to each other.

3. Plateau stage. This is the long middle period of the parental cycle. Most parents know that their children go through several developmental stages; they should realize that they develop, also, in parallel ways, as described in the literature by Dr. David Friedman.[5]

The child is an infant; the parents learn how to interpret his needs.

During the earliest months of a baby's life, the parents' most difficult problem is finding out what he is trying to tell them. The infant is physically helpless and his emotional involvement with his parents determines much of his future emotional health. Looking at this phase from the infant's point of view, Professor Erikson calls this "the period of trust."[6] The infant needs to establish confidence in his mother and in his environment, because this is a necessary foundation for all his future development. The parents need to establish confidence in their ability to understand the infant's needs and to respond to those needs, not only adequately but with ease and affection. They need to develop the capacity for empathy—understanding and joining in the infant's feelings. The ability to do this, which contributes greatly to both the parents' and the child's interpersonal relationships, has its beginnings in infancy.

The child is a toddler; the parents learn to accept his growth and development.

The parents now have to accept some loss of control over the child. The toddler becomes more mobile and begins to assert his independence, his first ideas about his own individuality and willpower. Erikson calls this "the period of autonomy,"[7] since it represents the earliest development of self-reliance and self-control. The parents, who up to this point have been caring for a helpless infant, now need to accept the child's growth and begin to "let go" while the child vacillates between dependence and independence.

The child is a preschooler; the parents as well as the child learn to separate.

Books on child-rearing discuss the separation anxiety that occurs in the two-year-old child. Often, however, parents do not realize that separation anxiety can be as difficult for them as it is for the child. Parents are told to allow the child to assert himself, to explore, to show initiative; at the same time they have to set limits and be present when the child needs them. They can become very confused and frightened because the child no longer seems to need them so much. But the child imitates them, and when they are able to accept the separation, so can he.

The child goes to school; the parents learn to accept rejection without deserting.

The child needs to fit into his peer group and move away from his parents, often ignoring them. This is the time of "industry" or "work completion," when he learns to win recognition by producing things and performing tasks set by teachers or peer-group members. The social life of the child gives rise to an inner discipline, and he may develop a strict conscience in his attempts to control his aggressive and sexual drives.

Parents need to give support unobtrusively during this phase without feeling hurt, disappointed, or angry. They must respect the child's feelings and his pride. Parents who need to be reassured of the child's faithfulness are the unhappiest people in the world. They experience the child as an extension of themselves and are more outer-directed in their values. They have, so to speak, put all their eggs in one basket. If the child is considered highly by other people, they experience a rise in self-esteem. If the child exhibits limitations in achievement, their self-esteem falls. If the child is successful and moves away from the parents through his successes, they experience rejection and a loss of self-esteem. Separation anxiety needs to be overcome both by parent and child.

The child is a teenager; the parents must learn to build a new life.

The adolescent's great struggle is to find himself, his own identity. In recent years cultural changes have made this task more difficult than ever. The peer group often becomes more important than the parents (or any other adult authority). Parents find it difficult to confine themselves to specific issues that can realistically be seen by the child as necessary and important. It is difficult to respect the young person's feelings and to avoid constant criticism or disapproval so as not to undermine morale and the parent-child relationship. Teenagers need to separate themselves from their parents.[8]

The parents must now start to rebuild their own lives. Success in their own self-development makes it possible for them to give support and help as needed without intruding on the adolescent's growth, and to relinquish control gradually as their child becomes more mature.

Socionormative factors

The description of the child as a teenager raises the issue of the accelerated rate of change in our society. Fundamental changes toward greater urbanization and geographic mobility are changing the nature of societal institutions, including the family. The family has shrunk in size, from the extended family with many relatives of an earlier day to today's comparatively isolated nuclear family. This has increased the burden of parenthood and intensified the difficulties of child-rearing. Today's parents and their children have grown up in markedly different worlds. The generation gap—generational differences in cultural values, knowledge and outlook—thus tends to be widened. If parents look only to their own experiences for guidance in understanding their children's needs, they are almost bound to encounter frustration, bewilderment, and disappointment. As a consequence of their exposure to concerns of their own adolescent children, many parents today have undertaken an agonizing reappraisal of their own attitudes and beliefs in the face of social change.

4. Disengagement stage. This stage leads up to and includes the end of the active parental role, which is generally considered to be up to the point of the child's marriage, although the time varies greatly and may in reality never come. Some people, unfortunately, try to force their active role as parents all their lives or are forced to continue it by circumstances (as in the case of retarded or physically handicapped children) even though they wish termination of their responsibility.

How parents grow

The goal of adolescence is maturity, both physical and psychological, but as we have seen, a person's emotional and psychological growth does not come to a stop at the age of twenty. He continues to grow and develop as a human being. When the individual is physically mature enough to have a child and psychologically mature enough to gratify both the child's needs and his own, he is ready to become a parent.

People do not grow only by advancing in a straight line, with never a backward glance—more likely, they grow in spirals. Starting in the present, they move ahead a little, gain new knowledge or understanding, then circle around, consider what has happened before, and integrate the old with the new. The psychological motion is spiral rather than straight. The past and the future are always acting on each other. Recognition of this pattern can prevent unnecessary anxiety.

Parenthood is a big step forward that requires much reconsidering of the past. In the process of learning to be a mother, a woman reexperiences what happened to her when she was being mothered. As she cares for her child, she can feel satisfied that she is taking good care of the child and can develop into an even more capable person; or she can feel frustrated and unhappy about her lack of ability and slip backward to a lower level of functioning. Just as the infant gains confidence and self-esteem through a good mother-child relationship, so does the mother.

Even though one does not remember all of it consciously, everyone has a host of feelings toward what happened in one's own childhood: whether the family was happy or not; whether its members felt confidence, acceptance, and love, or whether the predominant feelings were rejection and insecurity. As a parent cares for his own children, many of these old feelings come up again. This is normal, the way it is supposed to be. In each period of the child's growth, the parent reworks what happened to him many years ago. He turns back in the spiral. Hopefully, he then returns to a higher point—most people do. But some cannot resolve the conflicts and so fall back to a lower level of functioning or start to show symptoms of mental illness. This is an attempt to cope with the problem by compromise formation and is not within our focus of interest here.

The child acts as a mirror for his parents. They see themselves in the child. If his behavior expresses positive aspects of the parents—if he is loving, happy, intelligent, creative—his parents feel that these qualities are reflections of their own. They feel satisfied with what they have done thus far and more able to go on successfully. But when the child expresses negative aspects, the parents feel shocked and threatened.

All children, for example, whine and fuss occasionally. The books on rearing children indicate when this behavior is likely to occur, how much is normal, how much is a symptom of personality problems, and how the child should be treated in order to get him through the "fussy stage" with lasting gain but without lasting damage. What has not been dealt with so much in the literature is the effect of all this on the parents. It is natural for parents to be upset: "My child must have learned this from me! Do I really whine and complain like that?" Some parents will deny that the child could possibly have learned this from them. Others can use their feelings of shock and threat to change and develop into more mature individuals.

On the other hand, the child's idealization of his parents increases their self-esteem. This is seen in the father's response to the admiration of his son or the flirtation of his daughter, the mother's pleasure at her daughter's femininity and her son's love. But many people have never solved completely the conflict they may have felt over their own sexual attachment to their parents, they may still feel concern and guilt about conflicts originating many years before. When the child reaches that period, the parent works through his old conflicts again, this time from the viewpoint of an adult. A successful relationship with his child will help him to fuller acceptance of himself and the nature of human sexuality.

Every person carries with him not only those events that have happened in the past but also those that he hopes will happen in the future. Becoming a parent reactivates many old conflicts and arouses many new hopes of which the individual is barely aware or not at all aware. Parents rarely ask themselves, "What can we do to rear a child who will become the kind of adult we and the society value? What is the best way for us to integrate our role as parents with all the rest of our roles as adults?" Yet they operate under the pressure of such conflicts and questions, react to them, and are influenced by them. As indicated, pressures that peak at late adolescence, at the time for separation between the parents and their children, are heightened in a society undergoing rapid change.

References

1. James E. Anthony and T. Benedek, Eds, PARENTHOOD: ITS PSYCHOLOGY AND PSYCHOPATHOLOGY (New York: Little, Brown & Co., 1970).
2. *Ibid.*
3. K. Gibran, THE PROPHET (New York: Alfred A. Knopf, 1965) p 17.
4. Alice S. Rossi, "Transitions to Parenthood," *Journal of Marriage and the Family* 30:1, 1968, pp 26-39.
5. David Friedman, "Parent Development," *California Medicine* 86:1, 1957, pp 25-28.
6. Erik H. Erikson, CHILDHOOD AND SOCIETY (New York: W. W. Norton & Co., 1950) pp 219-224.
7. *Ibid.*
8. Group for the Advancement of Psychiatry, NORMAL ADOLESCENCE: ITS DYNAMICS AND IMPACT, GAP Report No. 68 (New York: The Group, 1968).

2

EXPECTATION AND DISAPPOINTMENT IN PARENTHOOD

People do things for many different reasons. Their past experiences, their basic needs, the society around them—all play a part in motivation. Psychologists now know a great deal about the forces, particularly in the past, that drive people, but have learned less about the expectations that lead people. One way or another, expectations are involved in all behavior. At supper time we decide what to eat, partly on the basis of being hungry but also on the basis of an expectation of how a particular food will taste. When our expectations are realistic, we leave the table with a satisfied feeling. But sometimes we have overestimated the cook or the dish, and we end up hungry and disappointed.

Expectation is an essential part of existence. It involves such important aspects of personality as faith and hope—ingredients essential to human life. But hand in hand with expectation goes a certain amount of disappointment.

The relationship between them is a very important one to parents, for it affects the feelings they have about themselves and their children and influences how they act toward their children. Most of all, it determines how parents feel about having been parents as they look back in their later years.

The expectations that people have about parenthood are as varied as are their expectations about other life experiences. A great many of these expectations are conscious. Most people, when asked what they expect of parenthood, can say a good deal about it. At the same time, many of the expectations they don't discuss are partially or completely unconscious, and come out only in attitudes and behavior. The unconscious expectations are often the most important, because their unrealistic elements (and there are always some of these) may take a long time to be modified by the way things really are. The more effectively parents can unravel these unconscious expectations, the better they can fit together their expectations and their actual life experiences.

Common expectations of parents

Every parent has his own individual expectations. Some expectations, however, are particularly influential in determining the parent-child relationship.

Children as an extension of the parents. Children are often felt as an extension of their parents' lives, particularly the highly valued aspects. They express the parents' faith that life is worth continuing and that there is something in their own lives which should be carried on. Most parents hope their children will have the experiences that have made them happiest and will show the attitudes and abilities that they are proudest of in themselves. They want to take pride in their children, they feel that through their children their lives are extended into future generations. The child is thus a form of immortality for his parents. The child is the extension of the parent into the future, the parent's contribution to the progress of mankind.

This may not always be ideal from the child's point of view. Children struggle to grow up, to be themselves, to separate from the parents. Overly proud parents, or those who push to extremes the similarities between themselves and their children, may make the child's separation more difficult than it need be. Disappointment sets in when the child does not fulfill the parents' expectations. The children of baseball fans are not all natural athletes; beautiful mothers have awkward daughters.

A parallel and sometimes even more difficult situation occurs when the parent communicates to his child the feeling that because he himself cannot do a particular thing, neither can the child.

Sooner or later most children surprise their parents by turning out to be only themselves in some important respects, by revealing some qualities uniquely their own that differ from those of either parent. The ensuing disappointment varies in its severity and in the degree to which parents are aware of it. Humor, irritation, a sense of sadness may characterize a psychological process by which parents come to terms with their disappointment. Or it may be more serious. The parent who cannot see his child in any terms except as an extension of himself may reject the child or keep up a continual, futile attempt to change him. Both the disappointment and the way it is handled may be unconscious; the parent may never connect his own feelings and actions with his unfulfilled expectations unless he happens to give his disappointment serious thought. This process of high hopes followed by disappointment sets up a mechanism for loss of self-esteem and feelings of depression.

Children as a second chance. Everyone has regrets. There are always personal failings that haunt us. We all have deficiencies, insecurities, and frustrations we wish we could correct. Besides hoping that children will carry on their best qualities, fathers and mothers often expect their children to make up for what they feel is lacking in themselves.

Parents' misconceived expectations include the hope that children will offer them a chance to heal old wounds and try a second time. The father who attributes the unhappiness of his life to lack of education will do anything to see his son get a college diploma whether he wants it or not. The mother whose life has been clouded by financial worry wants her daughter to marry a "financially successful" man and have an easier life than she has had. In so willing, she focuses on one factor and ignores all other considerations. Parents who grew up without brothers and sisters, or who had no close ties to their parents, sometimes want a large family full of companionship and friendly activity. The youngest in large families, distressed by fighting, jealousy, and lack of privacy, look forward to having one or two children and a peaceful, noncompetitive family life when they become parents.

Such expectations may be largely fulfilled. Things may work out the way the parents hoped, and disappointment may be kept to a minimum. More often—especially when expectations are very great—the reality falls short in some way and parents have to cope with definite disappointment. Here the wound may be double. If children fall short in areas where the parents are satisfied with themselves, at least self-satisfaction remains. But if the child fails to make up for an earlier frustration, then this is a second blow to the parents. The danger is that this kind of double disappointment will make it extremely difficult to accept children on their own terms. How does one accept children for themselves? This was dealt with in Chapter one: "And though they are with you they belong not to you."

A common reaction to the threat of disappointed expectations is to pressure children to achieve. Some parents push scholarship; others, athletic prowess. Society in recent years has reinforced such pressure. The post-sputnik anxiety about American schools has resulted in breakneck acceleration of the curriculum. Moreover, through Little League baseball, Pee Wee hockey, and Pop Warner football many children are seduced or coerced into early professionalism and fierce competition. In any case, parents who feel compelled to have their children make up for their own disappointments by exacting achievement from the child are tacitly encouraged by the larger community. The result is the death of childhood and a generation of children many of whom are prematurely sophisticated and harassed; for whom learning and sports are completely serious business, devoid of joy in the activity for its own sake; or who may drop out in reaction against such pressures, electing rather to remain permanently unsophisticated in the face of expectations they cannot possibly meet.

Is peace always possible? A third expectation of family life which parents reveal concerns the unrealistic belief that the normal situation is one in which there is no trouble. The logical extension of this misconception is that when there is trouble, someone or something has gone wrong. We resent upheaval as an intrusion on the peace and quiet we accept as "normal"—despite the fact that peace and quiet are often disrupted. Many people think that family life by its nature should consist only of love between parents and children that results in respect and appreciation. Supposedly, an average day is one in which any moments of disagreement or irritation are quickly resolved by talking and by good humor, without high-pitched emotional involvement. Rivalry between brothers and sisters is thought to be superficial and leavened by basic loyalty and companionship. Supposedly, parents are mature and selflessly involved with their children through their love for each other and their desire to do the best they can for their children.

These misconceptions have been enormously reinforced by the deluge of writing purporting to advise parents how to do better by their children. The assumption underlying most of this literature is the one we have been discussing: Family life ought to be peaceful, and if there is upheaval something has gone wrong which can (and should) be corrected by greater effort or wisdom on the part of the parents. The amount of parental guilt and anxiety generated by this idea is incalculable. It is unfortunate and ironic, because there are scientifically sound but rarely discussed reasons why family peace is *not* always possible. Because of the nature of parenthood things cannot go smoothly for very long. Periods of relative peace or relatively tension-free states are attainable and such times are deeply appreciated by children, are remembered fondly when they become adults as the happy, carefree days of childhood. Fortunately, however, such situations have a positive value—a certain amount of tension stimulates growth. We are not saying that every conflict or period of turbulence in family life is of little significance and therefore does not need examination. We do say that parents need a double awareness that family life, by its very nature, cannot be wholly smooth, without some rough spots, and that not every stormy occasion is the forerunner of an oncoming tornado.

The earliest expectation. The earliest and perhaps most critical expectation of all is that of birth itself. Since this phenomenon is unaccompanied by knowledge of what one is producing, one's expectations boil up to a very tension-filled moment until, with the birth of the child, the product becomes obvious. The common experiences around the birth of the baby are joyous ones for the nuclear and the extended family. Here, overestimation of the love object is seen to an extreme. At this critical point, the relationship of parents to child is often made or broken, and many children are either highly accepted or highly rejected, to the extent that this earliest attitude may continue for years.

Reactions of parents to children

The basic difficulty for parents is that children are childish, and their immaturity is a powerful stimulus for the parents in turn to react in a childlike manner. This may seem an odd reaction to those who think that children pattern themselves on the maturity of their parents, as of course they do. Children tend strongly to imitate and identify with their parents, or at least with many of their outstanding traits. As in physics, however, where every action calls forth an equal and opposite reaction, so in child-parent relationships the child (especially the infant) acts as a magnet to draw the parent into the orbit of immaturity.

The simplest, most obvious example is the way adults bill and coo and make fools of themselves over children. Although we enjoy the foolishness, there is an edge of disapproval to our enjoyment, for the adult has temporarily accepted a return to childhood behavior and what appears to be childishness makes other adults nervous.

Deeper and less obvious examples of return to earliest behavior are more complex. Consider the reaction of both parents to the infant in the earliest stage of life. Some infants are placid, others tense and irritable, but all are a round-the-clock responsibility. They require care, attention, and concern, and having to supply constant life-sustaining care drains both parents, physically and emotionally. While the father may be a help or a hindrance, in our society the mother usually is chiefly responsible for the infant's care. However, fathers, members of the extended family, and mothers' aides or substitutes also parent the young. In doing so they need the ability to empathize, to feel things as though they were the child. Another kind of remembrance is also involved by which they are tuned in to the touch, the smell, the appearance of the child. They feel his distress with themselves and with themselves enjoy his comfort and satisfaction. How they react to this feeling depends to a great extent on their own early experiences. If the child's distress is unpredictable and is associated with physical discomfort, they will feel upset by it, will be awkward in attending to the child's needs and unconsciously envious of his comfort. They may be too anxious to pace themselves according to the infant's schedule. If their own early experiences were pleasant, on the other hand, they will be better able to recreate with the baby the good experiences they themselves had. They will feel that the baby's discomfort is manageable and not overwhelming, and they will enjoy the change in his mood from distress to peace that results from their care.

Thus the temporary excursion back to childhood that is set in motion by the baby's needs may have both pleasurable and painful consequences. Since no infancy is perfectly blissful or without periods of distress, every mother carries some unpleasant reminders of her childhood and experiences some anxiety as she slips into childhood with her infant.

Moreover, though infantile demands can be met in the short run, they recur. The only solution to the baby's constant demand for care is for him to mature from infancy to childhood and then to adulthood. There are times with even the "easiest" baby when both parents have to walk the floor in shifts. Though desired, peace is not always possible. But if they believe that it is and that they as parents have failed with every breach of quiet, their morale sags. The mother's self-esteem particularly is tied in with her care of the infant. If things go badly with the child, she feels that she is a failure. She may become anxious, defensive, or resentful of the child, herself, her husband, or other convenient object.

The mother's reactions are the most obvious, since she is directly in contact with the child. But the father is involved, too. The relationship between husband and wife is readjusted when they become parents, as regards their relationship both with each other and with their child. Even when the balance is reestablished, it has its ups and downs. For instance, when the baby has colic, the mother feels she may have done something wrong, she must spend more time with the baby, taking him to the doctor, changing his formula, holding him, worrying about him. Somehow the baby always seems to need the most attention at dinnertime, when the husband's needs are greatest. Her concerns for the baby make it harder to take care of her husband. Although he also is concerned about the baby, he may feel neglected, may find fault with his wife on some other issue; feeling doubly criticized, she experiences even more anxiety and guilt. Each one feels that something is terribly wrong. But what is really wrong is their original expectations. Husband and wife expected that their life together could be forever peaceful, that any disturbance is abnormal, that anything less than perfection is proof of their own failure.

Problems due to the child's dependency are most common

early in infancy, but they are present throughout the life of children. As children grow up, they present other kinds of problems and may again involve their parents in other forms of regression to childhood. From ages two to four, for example, the issue is control of aggressive energy. At that age children become very active and intrusive. They get into everything and they push everyone to see how much of the world (including their parents) they can manipulate and control. Their ways of attempting control include tantrums, saying no, and going off on their own in certain limited but provocative ways.

The parents' task in this situation is to help the child control himself, his anger, and his behavior. The temptation is to be drawn into the excitement of the child's provocation and to respond in kind with a fury that is rationalized as the only possible way to control the child. Psychiatrists and psychologists have long known that aggression and violence can generate a special kind of excitement and longing to participate. Experience with the effects of mass communication and with rioting has recently helped the public to understand this phenomenon. In the home there is a fine line between the judicious use of force to control unreasonable behavior and the gratification of indulging in uncontrolled rage at the out-of-hand child. The line is as difficult to draw in such a situation as it is in the confusion of a campus riot.

The sense of having won but lost which overtakes the enraged parent when he has administered a furious spanking reflects his awareness that he has regressed to the child's own level. For all parents, it is extremely hard to handle a provocative, out-of-control toddler without responding in kind. However the parent responds, the provocation itself disrupts the expected peacefulness of family life. It is extremely difficult to bear in mind that the disruption is an inevitable part of growing up and not a sign that something has gone wrong.

There is another kind of childishness that draws parents into childlike feelings and behavior. Many children are fascinated by their own and their playmates' bodies; they enjoy the power of forbidden words and love to talk about toilet functions. Some parents are frightened and repelled by this fascination, even though they may have read somewhere that this is a natural stage in development which should be managed without undue alarm. Other parents are as delighted as the children, and use their understanding of the "modern" approach to dwell upon body functions and increase the child's excitement by their own interest. Many parents experience a combination of disgust and fascination, as determined by their own childhood experiences when encountering these areas of growth and development. The forbidden excitement and guilt the parent felt as a child are reactivated by his child's discovery of his body. The result is a loss of the mature perspective that would help the child to master his obsession with body functions.

Joys and sorrows surrounding expectations

Still another temptation to which parents are exposed can disturb family life perhaps more than any other. Since children show physical and temperamental features of the families of both parents, they are easily identified with significant people in their parents' lives—say, one of the grandparents or one of a parent's siblings. It is usually a relative about whom there is substantial emotional conflict, with the conflict displaced onto the child and the old scenario reenacted.

For example, a physician's oldest daughter was sensitive, high-strung and emotional like her grandfather. Her father had always hated and feared his father's volatility and temper tantrums, which he regarded as evil and self-centered. But he had coped with his father's emotional demands by being a hard worker and helper and by developing a keen sensitivity to his father's moods. He could forestall the man's rage by anticipating his demands and altogether being a model son. His attitude toward his own daughter was suspicious and critical. Although he tried at times to appease her demands, more often he unloaded on her the resentment and anger that had been buried because of his fear.

The tendency to replay old fears and conflicts with new characters is a major burden of parenthood. Because it is often unwitting, it disrupts the peace of family life with bewildering frequency. Such returns to an earlier scene involving a relationship with an important person in childhood are hard to understand on the surface and parents often feel very guilty about them. If they stop to think, "Whom does the child remind me of? What conflicts out of the past am I replaying?" they can often get a clue to the source of their difficulty.

A variation on this theme of seeing features of members of the family in the child is the hurt of not seeing in him any aspects of oneself, one's mate, or one's parents. This happens more often than has been noted in the literature. Yet it should not be thought that all parental expectations are doomed to failure. Just as frequent are instances of fulfilled expectations and instances where the child goes far beyond the wildest expectations of the parents. Talents and abilities not noted in the parents often are shown by the child. These may appear in various areas as scholastic ability, musical ability, artistic talent, or athletic prowess. Or the child may be a child with a particularly happy disposition whose joy in life is a pleasure to observe. With these children, fulfillment of parental expectations or gratification beyond their fondest hopes leads to elation and parental confidence. Then the parent feels he has done a more than satisfactory job. Sometimes this self-satisfaction is well earned and well deserved. Sometimes an element of luck is involved. This is because a number of uncontrollable factors in rearing children are always present.

Benedek notes that, at first, when the child is beginning to speak, it is pure pleasure for the parents to participate in his baby talk, to observe the evolution of his language and enjoy how much more he knows than they expected.[1] Especially during the early years of verbal communication, parents respond to the spontaneous expressions of the child with a sense of gratification. They experience him as a lucky extension of themselves and their joy in parenthood is at a peak.

It is later, when the child's individuality emerges, forecasting its definite contours, that communication becomes less possible through empathy and disappointments play a greater role in the experience of parenthood.

Expectations in adolescence

We have chosen to discuss expectations in adolescence separately for two reasons: Parental disappointments seem to be greatest in this age group in our current American culture; and expectations of significant people in the adolescent's current environment play a part in determining his sense of identity as well as his behavior.[2] The parents, the peer group, and the community all indicate their expectations of success or failure. Confusion arises when the expectations of one are contrary to those of the others. Peer groups stimulate the devaluation of parental authority, causing many parents to confuse a rebellion in manners with a rebellion in morals and leading them to expect the worst. Some parents expect continuing dependence; others, premature independence. It is confusing to the adolescent when both expectations are indicated simultaneously. A parent may expect the adolescent's independence in money matters but his continuing dependence in making other decisions.

Around the issue of attending college, some parents expect the adolescent to accomplish vicariously for them or to compete successfully for them. Rebellion against such pressures again causes some parents to expect the worst. It is helpful if the parent does not lose faith in himself as a parent and in his child's potential. It is also helpful to expect the adolescent to behave consistently with society, to develop a reasonable degree of independence, to make educational and vocational choices within his competence and his interests, and to develop a healthy social and sexual identification. Optimistic expectations are often an expression of the parent's trust in himself, whereas pessimistic expectations may be feelings of distrust of oneself projected onto the child.

The dilemma of parenthood

The parent may be the best kind of person he is able to be, but the final product of parenthood is not entirely within his control no matter how much of his life he devotes to his children. This fact presents what might be called "The True Dilemma Theory of Parenthood." There is such a thing as a true dilemma—a situation that has no solution. Whichever choice you make among those available, the end result may fall short of your desire. Should it turn out as well as or better than your wishes, a fortunate turn of events, something beyond your control may have been the decisive factor giving it the final direction. There are no simple answers to the question how to rear a child who will meet his parents' expectations. There is no how-to-do-it recipe book for raising children. Many factors are involved, and many of them are beyond the parents' control. Even with a small problem that appears to be simple there may be no "right" or "good" answer—merely a choice. The choice must be made with no certainty that good consequences will outweigh bad ones. We care terribly whether they are good or bad, but the intensity of our wishes does not influence the outcome.

For example, a teenage boy resisted the continuance of his religious education. He attended parochial school after his secular schooling for the day. The work was difficult for him. He did not keep up with the class and he skipped class sessions. He was the type of child who wants to please his father so he would go to the school building but he could not stand the embarrassment of being found inadequate in his classwork and could not attend classes. Instead, he would wander through the building, engaging in friendly conversations. His father was continually pressuring him, hoping to see some of his own ambitions realized through the boy. After a long period of struggle, the disturbance created in the home was more than the mother could stand. She thereupon sought consultation. A detailed examination of the multiple factors in the home led to a professional recommendation that the boy be allowed to withdraw from this advanced education. A dilemma then faced the parents. If they allowed the boy to stop his parochial schooling, they were both giving up their hopes for his scholarship and they feared that a pattern of dropping out would be established in his character. If they forced him to continue, there would be daily confrontations and other disturbances. There was no good choice and they decided on the path of least parent-child friction—to allow him to grow up into what he could be rather than what they wanted him to be.

In light of this decision, the ending of the story is ironic. At the parochial school one of the teachers, who took a personal interest in the boy, chided him for dropping out. He proposed a plan. The boy would come into his current events class, which was an advanced class for the brightest students, but he would not have to attend the "difficult" classes in which he was failing. This arrangement was an individual choice by a teacher who liked teaching and it was made without administrative sanction. The boy respected the teacher, wanted his approval, and accepted the plan. It should be noted that the boy knew he was not being forced to continue and could make a genuine choice. Human lives are studded with many such unexpected turns of events, and only less than desirable choices are available, with unpredictable outcomes. The outcome may or may not be as favorable as the outcome desired.

Inner peace for parents

A distinction should be made between expectations and rewards. Parents may feel that they deserve a reward from the process of being a parent. Parents who desire and expect such a reward are disappointed when they do not get it. It is not only children who need to be loved; the need for parents to be loved by their children merits recognition but is often underplayed. Creative literature is filled with stories of ungrateful children—as in *King Lear*—who bit the hand that fed them.

Enjoyment of the child as he is and a realization of what can be expected from him offer the parent opportunities for gratification rather than the disappointment attending unrealistic expectations. Inner peace, if this is a parent's expectation, comes from the father's or mother's development of his or her own inner resources rather than from the child's fulfillment of parental expectations. Ideally, a parent should strive to become as free as possible from his own childhood-determined expectations, so that there will not be too great a discrepancy between his expectations of his children and the way they really develop.

References

1. James E. Anthony and T. Benedek (eds), PARENTHOOD: ITS PSYCHOLOGY AND PSYCHOPATHOLOGY (New York: Little, Brown & Co., 1970).
2. C. Knight Aldrich, "Expectations: Great and Otherwise," *Wisconsin Medical Journal* 62:114-118, 1963.

3

MAINTAINING, CHANGING, AND TRANSMITTING VALUES

Difficulties encountered in transmitting values

The psychology of values is always a difficult area for psychiatrists. Shifting one's ground from the inner psychological forces to the outer social forces lends confusion. A deeper understanding of the issues involved in values derives from an interlocking of societal and family values, but this is a difficult task to accomplish. For psychiatrists, dictation of values and morals is not readily entered into. Not that this is unfamiliar territory. Working with superego, or conscience, is a daily activity. But analytic psychotherapy places the greatest amount of freedom and autonomy for personal growth in the hands of the individual. It seeks to foster the development of autonomy by scrupulously avoiding the introduction of extraneous attitudes. Respect for the other person's rights and freedom of choice is a foundation stone for the therapeutic approach. While telling other people what they should or should not do is inconsistent with this approach, clarifying alternatives among which the individual can choose is respectful of his human dignity. Furthermore, values cannot easily be changed by exhortation. They are deeply embedded in the personality, anchored in strong feelings.

It is probable that, for parents, establishing a moral climate in the home represents the task most accompanied by inner uncertainty and insecurity. There are many reasons for this. One is that the parents' values are constantly changing as experiences change with each new stage of growth and development. Moreover, as values of his society change, the parent is pressured to change his own established values.

Another source of confusion concerning conscience is that it has different meanings for different people. The religious person may claim that conscience is the voice of God and even assert that it must always be obeyed. A cleric may state that conscience is the human capacity or instrument for hearing what God says but that utilization of this human capacity can at times be blocked by ignorance or misinformation. Others consider conscience as a set of values transmitted from one generation to the next. The process of transmitting these values also transmits prejudices, so that the adult needs constantly to reevaluate and reassess his values in the light of new experiences and information.

Another difficulty in establishing a stable, enduring, easily transmittable set of values is our tendency not to practice what we preach. Parents tend to communicate double messages to children. If what the parent says and does are consistent during the formative years of the child, a conflict within the conscience will not be evident. If, in addition, this is consistent with what the child perceives in his experiences with his culture, he will develop into a stable, well-balanced person. No culture, however, is free of contradictory and conflicting value systems and contrary activities. Parents must work with such conflicting forces to establish and maintain their own values before they can function adequately as parents in transmitting them to the child. We must also recognize that a two-way system (even though biased in one direction) exists in that moral values are also transmitted from children to parents. At each stage of development the child's moral dilemmas stimulate a reworking of the parents' position on each issue.

Parents must establish their own values

The concern of this report with parents requires an emphasis upon the parents' inner values before the area in which they transmit these to their children can be examined. Some of these values have been delineated in preceding pages. In the Introduction, the value of lifelong personal growth and development was presented as giving an important meaning to life. In Chapter one, we discussed the value of successful separation of self and child resulting in two equal and adequate adults. This is achievable despite the fact that parenthood as a psychobiological process ends only with the death of the parent. In Chapter two, the value of continuing realizable expectations for oneself was recommended in place of expectations from one's children. In this chapter, the values recommended for achievement and maintenance through the parenting experience (in keeping with Erikson's model) are integrity, wisdom, and a feeling of kinship with mankind.[1] From his empathic experiences with children, the parent can move further toward humanitarian values.

The need for a high valuation of children

A primary value is a high value of children, an effective concern for children's needs. With such a concern parents can firmly establish their identity as parents, hopefully free of concerns about their rewards or their own reputation and status.

The parents most secure in their status as individuals are those most capable of demonstrating that the most valuable asset of the human race is its children. Without jeopardizing, and even adding to, their own integrity, parents can accept the value that children are the future and that it is their foundation years which set the stage for later life.

In March 1972, the American Medical Association sponsored a National Congress on the Quality of Life, which expressed such a high value of children in the keynote address of Mr. Hugh Downs:

> Whatever she is, I want my mother's body to be a fit factory for building my own. I want her mind to be free of oppres-

> sion and able to want and to care for me, and to love me as I will one day come to love her. Whatever race I am born to, for the sake of all races, I want my home to be secure enough that no feeling of hopelessness or myth of inferiority will be passed to me, I want the chance to learn what I will need to learn in order to grow. . . . Under whatever kind of government I am born, I want equal justice under which I will forge my own freedom.

Other values were expressed during the conference, for example:

> When a child arrives, wanted or not, [he] requires love and encouragement to realize his own destiny. . . . Parents should develop curiosity about their child . . . make their own values very explicit to children . . . enhance self-concepts and confidence by guiding the child . . . help the child develop individuality . . . provide an atmosphere of psychological safety and support which makes it possible to live amid tensions from many sources.

Whether any culture truly values children above adults is open to question. Certainly our society has never provided even as adequately for children as have the socialist countries or Germany, and currently it is reducing the wherewithal for child care, be it in the form of education, day-care centers, remedial programs, or health services.

In the preceding chapters we have focused upon the continuing growth and development of the parent into a mature individual. In this chapter, we add another dimension—the development of his character—which includes a value system that considers the needs of the child to be of utmost importance without requiring the parent to feel personally depleted thereby.

Values that contribute to the child's character

Morality defines values and the behavior that is appropriate in a particular situation; it guides the individual in governing his actions. Morality is much more than a series of prohibitions. In an individual who is growing in a healthy manner, the inner controls are strengthened and pulled together, they take on a guiding and sustaining role in conduct and in human relationships. Morality is a basic mechanism that directs a person's life, integrates his personality, and allows him to live harmoniously with others despite the population density of our modern society.

Among the many tasks of growing up that a parent helps his child to accomplish, two relate particularly to values: developing his internal controls and constructing an individual moral philosophy. In helping his child, the parent must work on the same problems within himself—successfully or unsuccessfully. The parent may thus strengthen or weaken his inner integrity and functioning. The child has to learn to live with heightened impulses and to find a balance between desire and restraint. The parent helps his child to build a system of values that will serve as a guide to conduct and the incorporation of values in his own particular circumstances. He helps the child construct a working system that will be his own and not just a rigid imitation of what he has been taught to believe. In this process of moral development, the child develops character.

One of the controversies between differing philosophies of education is whether the educational system should or should not contribute to the family's role with a school program to develop the child's character. Working societies need a common core of accepted values to give character cohesion and minimal stability. This country has had such a core of values, which seem to be losing their powers in the face of rising crime rates, incivility, shoddy work, and lack of personal discipline. Some educators have advocated that American education commit itself to a program of developing character through textbooks and other readings which, by story and historical example, illustrate the moral lessons all children should learn. They know that there would be strenuous objections to "indoctrination of middle-class values into students," but believe them to be sound and broadly applicable. They feel that any society which does not have enough self-confidence in its fundamental values to instruct the young in them, or enough common sense to do so, is courting disaster. The values they would inculcate are: honesty and truthfulness, trustworthiness, joy in work well done, kindness and compassion, the courage to admit mistakes, racial tolerance, respect for law, nonviolence in pursuit of one's goals, and respect for democratic rights.

How many parents could pass this test?

Parents' contributions to morals

The parent contributes to three significant areas in which a young person explores values, tries out his controls, and searches for the type of person he and his parents want him to be: religion, social idealism, and sex.

1) Religion. The adolescent, as part of his movement toward independence, examines the religious beliefs given him by his family and his culture. He may discard certain of the religious beliefs of childhood as he searches for his own set of values and his own identity. He compares his religious beliefs with those of his peer group members. (This process usually involves some change, but it can result in anything from abandonment to renewed intensity.) In order to become fully emancipated from his parents, the adolescent usually needs to doubt their religious attitudes, values, and standards. For his part, the parent cannot help being affected by these activities of the child. To some degree, he is forced to reassess his own religious attitudes, values, and standards during both the spoken and the nonverbal communication with his questioning, growing offspring.

Often, the child's rebellion is against what he *thought* was taught him, not what he actually was taught. Sometimes, however, his rebellion is directed against what he was taught as it differed from what was practiced. In general, he is basically rejecting not a mature religious belief but his own childhood conceptions. Many years may pass before he realizes that his rebellion was not so much against parents, church, or culture as against his own immaturity. Nevertheless, few things are so upsetting to parents as an adolescent, struggling with the task of emancipation, who attacks their treasured value system. It may shake his parents' confidence in his knowledge of reality and cause them to feel their child is obnoxious.[2]

To carry out this process of testing and questioning their religious beliefs, adolescents first need to be exposed to some structure or order of religion or humanistic values. There are parents who are not religious but who need to transmit such values. Many parents feel they are doing the child a favor in not presenting specific religious beliefs, or they expose him to a number of different beliefs in the hope that he will as he matures pick out the ones he wants to keep. But it may well be that obscurity or permissiveness in matters of religion gives the adolescent nothing to rebel against or to depend upon. It is as though he wanted something crisp and exciting to chew on and was given vanilla pudding instead. We are proud, in our society, of our great tolerance and of the fact that we permit many different kinds of religious values and beliefs to coexist. But in such a society the adolescent's religious conflicts may not be so easy to resolve as they are in a society with a more structured set of values and points of view. In a more dogmatic society, at least, he knows what he is fighting.

The stage indicated in the following episode is particularly difficult for parents to weather with a sense of perspective. One Sunday morning at breakfast, a psychiatrist's adolescent son announced that he had become an atheist. He had previously considered the ministry as a vocation. About the same time another physician's son, who had also considered the ministry, announced *his* atheism to his family. The two boys, it turned out, were friends and had been discussing religious matters with each other. Both sets of parents were deeply troubled. They wondered what had happened to their sons and what they had or had not done to cause such an about-face.

This stage of atheism is fairly common in adolescence—agnosticism would probably be a better word for it. It usually involves the young person's relationship to both his father and the being he calls God. In the small child, the religious experience is closely bound to his experiences with his parents. God is thought of in essentially the same way as father. The father might be for the child his picture of God. The same pattern is seen with the child's conception of important figures.

If the young person's development proceeds normally, he learns to separate the two; he sees his parents as less divine and more human, while God becomes less identified as his father. This separation is one of the tasks of adolescence; in the process the adolescent may reject God or father or possibly both. This is a normal but usually transient phenomenon. Even when of relatively short duration, however, it is trying and perplexing to the parents. As he works through his rebellion and gains a firmer idea of his own identity, the child arrives at a new relationship with both God and father. He is then free to use religious beliefs in an appropriate and constructive manner.

2) Social idealism. During the inner struggles of adolescence, social concerns are often an important part of the young person's life. The reasons for human existence are heatedly debated and the desire to do something to improve the world is conspicuously present. Sometimes social concerns are blended with religious aspirations. As one might suspect, this religious-social idealism springs partly from the fact that the young person is going through a very turbulent period during which he projects his inner turmoil onto the world outside. "Everything is in chaos," he thinks. "I've got to do something about straightening it out!" He does not realize that a great deal of the chaos is inside himself.

Upheaval in the outer world makes the inner conflict more intense than it might otherwise be. In a time of great social change the work of adolescence becomes much more difficult. A stable environment helps greatly to provide an anchor, and even more important than a stable physical environment is a stable emotional one. In a recent study carried out with a hundred college students, a number of them spoke of conflicts related to social and religious issues. Hypocrisy was one of the features that caused them pain and confusion. They were especially distressed by the efforts of "religious" adults to twist religious teachings in order to justify their particular hates, prejudices, or bigotry. These students stated that they would have been less shaken had the adults acknowledged religious precepts as ideal, at the same time admitting their inability to attain that ideal in all their actions. Twisting and distorting the structure of religious idealism left them with no fixed point by which to orient their values or their conduct.[3]

In the young person's search for inner harmony nothing is more helpful than an adult example of mutual understanding, cooperative living, and devotion to the principle of equality for all human beings. Respect for personality, regard for the rights and feelings of others, and commitment to the common good are ethical values that the young person can hold onto and see as functional and valuable while he sorts out his own beliefs and modes of action. Here again, the child unknowingly gives the parent an opportunity for reassessment and personal growth.

The opposite of social idealism involves the phenomenon of prejudice and its transmission from parents to children. The best definition of prejudice is probably the popular, informal "Prejudice is being down on something you're not up on." It is similar in meaning to a more formal definition by Thomas Aquinas: "Thinking ill of others without sufficient warrant." The variables involved in prejudice are hostility and ignorance or erroneous judgment.

Parental involvement in children's prejudices emerges in a variety of ways. In the most direct way, the negative feelings and biases about certain individuals and groups are expressed by precept and example in the presence of children. Both the personality structure of the parents and the atmosphere in the home contribute to the open-mindedness or prejudice of the children. For example, in a revealing study of prejudice among children at the sixth-grade level, it was found that some of the children were extremely prejudiced and some were not. The investigators asked the mothers of these children questions about their child-training practices without revealing their specific reasons for the interview. They found a very significant difference between the philosophy of child training motivating the two groups. The prejudiced children had mothers who believed in firm punishment, including whipping, who believed that the child should not "talk back," and so on. On the whole, they were much more authoritarian than the mothers of the nonprejudiced children, who were more open, democratic, and benevolent in their approach to their children and to themselves.

Attitudes the child acquires in the home are blended with what he observes and experiences in the outside world. As parents observe the child's actions and listen to his ideas, whether negative or positive, they are forced to reexamine their own views and actions in the light of the value system they espouse.

3) Sexuality. Genital sex—the biological functions of male and female—is only a small part of complete sexuality, which is a person's whole identification as a man or a woman.

When the psychologist Erik Erikson analyzed the developmental tasks of adolescence and early adulthood, he put the development of individual identity before development of the capacity for intimacy. By this he means that a person must know who he is before he can share himself closely with another person. Unless his own identity is well established, intimacy may bring psychological fragmentation.

Society's intense preoccupation with genital sexuality has created both moral and identity problems for the developing child and confusion within the parent as to his responsibilities. Free sexual expression appears to be encouraged on all sides, with the implication that sexuality is the only form of identity that matters. A particularly dangerous aspect of this preoccupation is the exploitation of sex in order to sell merchandise. Segments of our society which attempt to control sexuality seem inadvertently to call undue attention to it. Many observers have pointed out that when a group insists on suppressing the sex instinct in everything, it betrays the fact that it really sees this instinct everywhere it looks.

Parents are often puzzled by the fact that young people link social consciousness and sexuality together. Nothing is more evident in the adolescent than a heightened sense of the erotic. Simultaneously he experiences a widening and deepening of the ocean of goodwill. The different types of love sustain, feed, and strengthen one another; the feeling of love that permeates a youth's life and helps him relate to the opposite sex is closely akin to his love for God and for other human beings. When he carries a sign saying "Make love, not war," his imperative may appear depraved to many adults. But is it? His involvement in social reforms and social action is not just a sublimation of his sexual drives, but rather an expression of those same powerful forces in a different area of his life. Most adults, on the other hand, draw a sharp dividing line between genital sexuality and social consciousness. Here the parent can learn from his adolescent child. Our fragmentation of the various approaches to love has made us miss the larger dimension of personal love, the totality with which love can engage the whole of one's personality. This has been a soul-searching experience for many parents.

Role models and sex education

In the past, the mother's role and the father's role in the family were clearly defined and quite separate. Few expected the father to help with the housework or the mother to earn a substantial portion of the family income. When these conditions did occur, the adjustment was seen as a response to an emergency or an inference was drawn that there was "something wrong" with the family and its members. Today, there is much more freedom to share parental roles. But children still need to learn from their family life that men and women do have different, complementary roles, that they need one another and need to take care of one another.

The child's understanding of sex roles as he learns them from his parents strongly influences his assimilation of what he learns about sex. The average child knows a good deal about sex, even when he does not receive formal sex education at home or in school. ("Sex education is nothing new," one teacher says to another. "We had it when I was going to school, but in those days we called it 'recess.' ") Though children today are less likely to suffer a sense of guilt and shame, they can still be disturbed and inhibited about sex. It is important for the parents to have a warm and loving relationship and to show the child that love and sex belong together. Sex instruction whenever given should be given in such a way that the child can recognize the relationship of sex to other experiences rather than think of sex as an activity separated from or even opposed to other aspects of living.

In their own communities many parents have taken part in some phase of the current battle over what type of sex education is suitable for children of various ages. There is a wide variation of opinion on this question even among experts. One complicating factor is that even if every child were to receive the same information in class, the parents' unspoken feelings will be conveyed to their children, so that the children from different homes will have very different emotional reactions to what they are learning. Many parents are embarrassed about sex, frustrated over their own less-than-perfect sexual adjustment, and disturbed over the new openness about sex (quite apart from any change in moral standards). Here again is an opportunity for parents, through their children, to work out solutions to a problem they actually share.

Most parents know they should answer children's questions directly, giving the information requested but not confusing the child with material for which he is not ready. They should discuss whatever topics come up with full attention and, hopefully, without embarrassment. Perhaps the most important part of sex education is not related to sex and reproduction *per se* but to the development of social values, self-respect, and respect for others. Without this overall personal development, free and uninhibited sex can easily be used in the service of unhealthy goals—for example, proof of power, exploitation of others, self-aggrandizement. Good sex education implies the achievement by the individual of sexual selfhood and the development of his capacity to use his sexuality creatively and responsibly in all his human relationships. Sex education is not just an academic subject but a psychodynamic process that should continue for a lifetime.

Further considerations of the development of conscience

Although the child must ultimately decide for himself his own set of moral values, the development of conscience does not occur in a vacuum. Conscience develops because the child identifies with significant persons in his life and follows their values. As he sees that these values are good for him, he absorbs them and makes them his own. Situations such as moving from one foster home to another, parents' divorce and remarriage, inconsistent discipline, serious physical maltreatment, or lack of love and emotional care make it extremely difficult if not impossible for a child to maintain a stable relationship with his parents or to accept their values.

Everyone, including parents, responds to new experiences. The child, because his personality is still in the process of being molded, responds more strongly than an older person, and stimuli have a more pronounced effect on him. The parent responds because his new responsibilities make him more sensitive to the new stimuli. We can think of every stimulus from the family environment as a message that both the child and the parent have to interpret. If the message is direct and clear, they receive it without confusion and act on it, but if they receive it at one level that is contradicted on another, they develop inconsistent and conflicting images that cause great confusion in the family.

The classic example is that of the person who says one thing and does another. But it is not just one person who is involved in the family. In illustration, a mother filched extra spending money for her son from her responsible, hard-working husband, and the boy knew it. He saw one important person in his life stealing and the other being honest. As an adult, he spent his life struggling between indulging himself illegally (as his mother had done) and being a responsible worker and family man (like his father). The confusion in values thus created caused guilt and ambiguity that lasted into adulthood.

Sometimes the confusion originates outside the family, since the child learns not just from his parents but also from the entire society around him. For better or worse, our society has adopted middle-class goals that portray the American dream of unlimited opportunity, material success, education, and status. At the same time, society denies children from the lower socioeconomic levels the chance to achieve those goals. Middle-class children learn the social ideals of "success." They learn also from their parents that they can and should achieve such success and are helped by the family to achieve it. In this situation the values are consistent.

On the other hand, youngsters from depressed groups find that society teaches them one thing and their own social group another. They have little direct contact with "successful" persons, they often lack an adequate family life, and they are not sure how to find legitimate ways of gaining recognition. Often their parents are bitter and hostile toward the middle-class world, which holds out ideals they cannot achieve; the children reflect this bitterness and hostility. In addition to coping with the conflict in values, they have to seek methods of gaining satisfaction, and since society will not give them the status they seek, they have to look outside it. They find groups with values they can realize but these values are often opposed to those of a stable society. For such children, status may depend on prowess in fighting, drug use, destroying lives or property, or taking by force or stealth what cannot be obtained legitimately.

Thus it is not always the parents' poverty or lack of education that is damaging to their children. It is rather the contradictions the children see in a society which says that everyone should have an education, sufficient income, an opportunity to accomplish as much as he can, and the training that will help him accomplish it, but which fails to provide what is necessary in order for them to attain these goals.

A contradiction likewise occurs when a child finds it necessary to identify closely not just with family, neighborhood, and city, but with a larger community such as the nation. A clear identification is difficult when a country describing itself as a democracy practices expediency, favoritism, or ruthlessness toward certain groups within the nation or outside it. A youngster may need to identify with his country while seeing its values as cruel, hypocritical, and destructive of individual freedom. He may then respond by asking, "If this is my country, I do not belong here, but where do I belong?" Such questioning may be more upsetting than questioning one's own ability to live up to those values.

A study of rebellion in college students

Not only the disadvantaged have these troubles; youngsters from all socioeconomic levels may have difficulty committing themselves to ordinary social values. Kenneth Keniston has studied in depth the puzzling phenomenon of a group of our brightest and most privileged youths who have come to despise and reject the society in which they have grown up and which has afforded them its best opportunities and advantages.[4] He found that they shared the experience of being raised in families in which the father, though often highly successful in his work and accepted as a person of accomplishment, had withdrawn from the demands of family life and particularly from those of his wife. She responded by becoming seductive and treacherous in her urgent need to extract at least minimal attention and emotional support from her husband and children.

The children reacted by hating and mistrusting the father for his weakness and fearing the mother's ability to use them against the father. They could not trust either parent. Because they had never trusted or identified with either parent, they were unable to identify with anyone else. Adulthood, in their view, meant committing oneself to people, institutions, and causes which they saw as making destructive claims on them. Adulthood meant accepting a state of awareness like that of their parents, accepting limitations on openness and genuineness, devotion to materialism, boring work, and control by the demands of others. Their disaffection was so deep-seated that it paralyzed them. "Strong in opposition, these young men are weak in affirmation; unable to articulate or even to know what they stand for, they have little sense of self to stand on. . . . But rebels without a cause can only stand against, not for; and even their opposition is diffuse and unspecific. The price they pay for this opposition . . . is inner confusion, disunity, and fragmentation." [5]

It should be noted that all protesters do not come from disturbed families. Some social inequities can be recognized because they are obvious. Such recognition can be a sign of healthy family values transmitted by parents. The other side of the coin is revealed in a study of 200 highly successful college students who were asked what in their background or life experience they felt had kept them on an effective, goal-oriented path.[6] The majority of respondents identified the family as the most important motivational factor in their lives, and they often commented on certain particular values. Among family characteristics reported were firmness, neither overly permissive nor rigid; direction without dictation; rules that made sense; high expectations of all family members; and mutual trust and respect. The parents had their precepts and lived up to them. This consistency of precept and practice was noted with appreciation.

All these students rebelled at times against the demands and value systems of their families, although rebellion was generally verbal and rarely took the form of acting-out or destructive behavior such as experimenting with drugs or quitting school. The home seemed to save them from severe identity crises, for they usually had a strong feeling of who they were and where they were going. Not all the students were close to their parents, but they were able to communicate and share their concerns, fears, and hopes. The parents were available when needed and gave generously of their time. For many of the students, the time their parents gave them seemed to outweigh in importance everything else they received.

Tied closely to the giving of time was the feeling communicated to them by the parents, "You are somebody." Thus they did not want to disappoint their parents; more importantly, their self-esteem and sense of worth seemed to push them toward fulfillment of their capabilities. The families of these students fell within a considerable socioeconomic range, from very modest earnings to great affluence, but values were similar despite vast differences in material resources.

In the young person's search for acceptable values, he needs to live in a state of creative tension regarding morality. The individual must continually balance and weigh his actions in terms of how he can put abstract principles into action within the context of his group's values and his own personal values. Morality can never be completely an individual matter, because of its necessary relationship to the group as well as to the individual, and the individual's behavior is integrated by his moral commitments to himself and to his society according to a whole range of social values.

These various demands upon a person's values always cause conflict and tension, always call for compromise and adjustment. Parents should temper their legitimate concern over value transmission with the realization that a child must test the values he has learned. He must see whether they really work; he must incorporate them into the pattern of what hc wants to do, rather than what he must do.

Summary

In conclusion, the role of the parent in the area of values is to establish a working set of values for himself. These values need not be "supermodern," or "loose-minded," but should be open-minded. Parents need not accept valuelessness as a way of life. They have a right and a duty to advocate particular values and expectations; they have the right to attempt to pass these values on to their children. They must, however, respect the child's right to go through a phase of living by contradicting values and to establish differing values on a permanent basis. His doing these things need not be seen as a negative reflection upon the parent. It is in the nature of the child-parent relationship and at times may reflect positively upon the parents' rearing of the child.

Communication, which is a positive value, can go a long way, but there may come a point when communication has to come to an end and action takes place. Consider, for example, the college girl who brought her boyfriend home and demanded that they be allowed to sleep together in her bedroom. It was within the daughter's values not to be hypocritical, and she was being true to herself in taking this position. Yet it was not within the mother's values to condone this behavior and she finally had to say (in order to be true to herself), "You may sleep with your boyfriend if you wish, but not in my house."

This example of holding the line can be an act of love. Parents should feel free to offer love, as well as direction and education. Love is a vehicle for the transmission of values. Children will use value systems to pressure parents to rebel, to relate to peer groups. It is essential for parents to uphold their own values in order to preserve their own self-integrity. Parents must also reexamine their own values, because throughout life the conscience undergoes modification in the same spiral-like fashion as emotional development. Commitment is essential to a full life. But, commitment is essentially a neutral term. One has to ask, "Commitment to what?"

References

1. Erik H. Erikson, CHILDHOOD AND SOCIETY (New York: W. W. Norton & Co., 1950) pp 219-224.
2. Peter A. Martin, "Obnoxiousness in Psychiatric Patients and Others," in *The Psychiatric Forum,* Gene L. Usdin, ed (New York: Brunner/Mazel, 1972) Chapter 9, pp 59-69.
3. James A. Knight, "Religious-Psychological Conflicts of the Adolescent," in ADOLESCENCE, CARE AND COUNSELING, Gene L. Usdin, ed (Philadelphia: J. B. Lippincott Co., 1967) pp 31-50.
4. Kenneth Keniston, THE UNCOMMITTED: ALIENATED YOUTH IN AMERICAN SOCIETY (New York: Harcourt, Brace & World, 1967).
5. *Ibid.*
6. James A. Knight, "Resisting the Call of the Cave," *Medical Insight* 2:66-77, 1970.

4

DISCIPLINE: SELF AND IMPOSED

Changing parental attitudes

The area of discipline is particularly exposing of difficulties within the parent. There is a tendency for parents to act out their own difficulties within the framework of administering discipline to their children. Every method has been tried by parents.

Recently, in the window of a Washington toy shop a large poster was placed which timed the changing "Advice to Parents" over the past sixty years. Though perhaps not completely accurate, it eloquently reflects some of the confusion felt by parents over how to train and discipline their children:

1910—Spank them
1920—Deprive them
1930—Ignore them
1940—Reason with them
1950—Love them
1960—Spank them lovingly
1970—THE HELL WITH THEM!

The anger expressed in the 1970 attitude may be seen as a cover-up or prelude to the despair and depression parents feel when they have lost confidence in their ability to succeed as parents. Another example of parental attitudes revealed through humor is the founding in 1972 of an organization call Parents Lib. The battle cry of this organization urges parents to commit themselves totally to the absolute severance of the umbilical cord, once and for all.

Life was simpler several generations ago, and most rights and responsibilities were more sharply defined for both parents and children. There was no question as to who was the authority—it was the parents, usually the father. Family life was simpler and more clearly structured, job and career possibilities were limited, and parents were seldom called upon for direction and guidance. Misbehavior could be dismissed by ascribing it to natural wickedness or the inheritance of bad traits, and every family had its "black sheep" who served the function of scapegoat. Little thought was given to the relationship between how a child was treated and how he behaved.

Childhood before the Enlightenment is so described in a book by David Hunt.[1] Hunt covers the late sixteenth and seventeenth centuries, limiting his field to the upper- and upper-middle-class families of France. This period has been characterized by the noted churchman Berulle as producing the meanest and most abject state of the human condition. Adults were not indifferent to children's needs but were not sympathetic to them. Adults were disturbed by aspects of the orality, obstinacy, and sexuality of their children. Breast-feeding was considered unhealthy for the mother, and child-rearing generally burdensome and unrewarding. Infants were frequently boarded out to rural wet nurses of the peasant and lower-class strata of society. Negative attitudes toward children as demanding and dangerous little animals prevailed.

This period in history followed the Middle Ages, when child-rearing attitudes were less constraining but more erratic. It was followed by the Enlightenment, characterized by increasing emphasis on intellectual achievement and independence.[2] The latter period, from the eighteenth century to the twentieth, was predicated on an entirely different home environment. It was like coming out of an ice age of parenthood with a melting of the glaciers. The emotional climate of the family in the past two hundred years "has become warmer, affectively sustaining, intellectually stimulating, and a breeding ground of neuroses."[3] These changes in the emotional climate of the family occurred first in the upper and middle classes and in time also in the working classes.

The predominant impetus in the socialization of the young in those early modern times was in the direction of training for unquestioning obedience and respect for authority, with corporal punishment not only given regularly but sometimes regarded as a sacred duty. Chastisement was designed to humble the child and to break his will. The prevailing philosophy was that a child must be motivated by threats and punishments to learn to behave himself, to acquire knowledge, and to become a useful member of society.

As the change took place toward warmth, affection, and respect for the rights of the young, the twentieth century came to be known as the century of the child. Today, with the increase in knowledge about how a person grows and learns, parents have an added burden. To parenthood has been added the awareness that parents' words and actions and what they are themselves can affect their children and the way their children act. The discipline of parenthood has grown to encompass many things: knowledge of how children grow and develop; the application of this knowledge; patience, tolerance, and fairness; flexibility, respect, and love.

The definition of discipline

The word *discipline* has many uses and many definitions: a method of training; a system of rules; a state of orderliness gained through self-control; punishment by someone in authority. Many people came to believe that the last definition was the only correct one. "Discipline" meant enforcing one's will upon a child by harshness and strictness, with the goal of obedience foremost. You made the child behave, and that was that.

Today we recognize that discipline (which comes from the Latin word *disciplina,* referring to teaching) involves more than this. Discipline is the process of organizing one's impulses for the attainment of self-control and self-direction. It is based on the parent's understanding of his children, on his knowing their strengths and weaknesses. And because it requires particular skills that must be learned along with self-direction and self-control, discipline embodies a twofold concept—not only the guidance and control the parent exerts on the child, but the inner self-guidance and self-control of the parent.

The practice of discipline

Without question, discipline is a natural and necessary tool for the parents of today who hope to raise happy, successful, and mature individuals. It is essential for their growth and security. No family, community, nation, or any other human society can run smoothly without a system of regulations and some means of enforcing them. No person can participate in any group without subjecting himself to control.[4] Children, especially, need to know that there are people in their lives who will interpret these controls and limits as clear and reasonable. Since children are really the disciples of their parents, they will learn from their parents' leadership and guidance, from the roles their parents play, and from their essential personalities. The terms *disciple* and *discipline* are connected, because, truly, to teach a disciple is to teach and act out discipline (for both teacher and student, parent and child).

The best discipline is that which leads the child from outer controls to inner self-control—to the desire for consideration of others and for appropriate ways of conforming to the outer world. Adults need to safeguard children from the consequences of those acts which are beyond their capacity to handle. In situations involving physical danger, in social situations they cannot yet judge for themselves, in circumstances where their uncontrolled aggressive feelings are aroused, children need to know that their parents understand, that they can and will set limits and control their childrens' behavior. Yet the load of really necessary restrictions in early childhood is so enormous that it is advisable to cut out every possible unimportant or artificial rule. Parents generally manage the child in the earliest years by example, positive suggestion, distraction, physical removal, leading, appealing to his desire to be grown up. As the child begins to sense what his parents do and do not want, the parents can rely more on verbal requests, realizing that at the same time they have to be reasonably consistent and must feel, speak, and act as though they expect to be obeyed.

Parental expectation in the area of discipline is a very important implementing force. The parent confident in his own authority expects appropriate response to his controls from the child, hence has fewer disciplinary problems. All other things being equal, the one the child loves and admires is the one the child obeys. It is the child's pleasure to give pleasure to those whom he loves and by whom he feels loved. However, there is one factor that complicates this tendency—the time spent with the child. The one who spends the most time with the child, the one on whose presence the child can depend even if not loved and admired, becomes the one who is obeyed and copied. Identification with the constantly present aggressor is commonly observed in young children. What is recommended here to the parent for the child's good is that he be considered by the parent as a person in his own right. The teacher must practice what he preaches.

This does not mean that the child will find the parent's limits easy to accept. He can learn quickly enough to distinguish between an act which is approved and one which is disapproved; the problem is getting him to *want* to do the right thing, rather than insisting that he follow a rule because of the consequences if he does not. Thus the child learns most easily when, because of his good relationship with his parents, he wants to please them. A relationship of trust and affection also keeps the parents sure enough of their child's love that they can act with objectivity. Parents need not fear that the child's every whim is an expression of need, nor need they feel frightened or guilty when they assert their authority or refuse to gratify a child's every wish.

Older children need parents who will stand behind them firmly with advice and guidance but who are mature enough themselves to give up authority gradually as the need for it passes. Little by little, control from without gives way to control from within, and the child is helped by the parent to accept increasing responsibility for his own behavior. In this process, the parent learns once more to accept increasing responsibility for his own behavior and inadvertently becomes a better model for discipline.

Whenever cause and effect are related clearly enough, parents can help the child see that what happens to him comes about through his own earlier behavior. This is sound learning technique. It is far more effective than controlling behavior consisting of parental threats, promises, or orders, which can never instill the internal orderliness gained from self-control or transmit a technique for coping with new situations.

Effects of the child on the parents

It would be appropriate here to stress a principle upon which the other chapters of this report are based. We must take into account the differences among children. Some of these differences can be recognized almost at birth. Not only are there innate psychological differences between infants, but they may be of such a kind and degree as to evoke very different responses from the behavioral repertoire of a given father or mother.[5] These innate differences (temperament) in the child can evoke negative or positive responses from his parents. Some children tend to be more passive than others and submit more readily than others. It would be well for parents to recognize that provocative behavior is often an attempt at mastery, a way of actively doing instead of passively submitting. Recognition of individual differences in children and of different responses from children to the same parental activity relieves parental guilt and anxiety and facilitates acceptance of the child as a unique individual.

Parents' attitudes are most important. Cold, rejecting parents may not have the most behavior problems with their children. But immediate peace is not the goal—long-term adult self-discipline is. If the child has no admired adult whose wishes he can utilize, he may not succeed in internalizing his controls. Other parents expect not to be able to control their children (perhaps they were allowed to get away with misbehavior when they were young). These parents become frightened and confused when forced to work through their own unsuccessfully handled problem in the area of controls. They cannot play the part of leader since their own inner controls are faulty, but must fight at the child's level rather than guide him. Again, where mother and father cannot work with each other to apply the same rules and maintain a consistent attitude, the child can never learn what is expected of him. He does not learn self-control, but he does learn the techniques for manipulating adults. If the rules are changeable, he reasons, so are the adults. His job, rather than learning how to behave within a system of rules, becomes that of learning how to get around his parents.

The attitudes of permissiveness

"Permissiveness" and "license" have become confused in the thinking of many parents. Such parents have interpreted recommendations for greater freedom and self-determination for children to mean they should do little or nothing to control their children. This situation can also prevail when parents become afraid of their children or are unwilling or unable to take a definite stand on anything. The children rule the home and get whatever they want.

Permissiveness involves accepting the childishness of children.[6] It allows them their own feelings, fantasies, thoughts, and dreams; it brings confidence and an increasing capacity to express feelings and thoughts. Permissiveness is necessary if the child is to develop his full potential without cramping or constriction.

But permissiveness is *not* the avoidance of necessary responsibility, of setting sensible limits and taking a stand on important issues. This is overpermissiveness, which blocks development of control and leads to rudeness and aggressiveness—all the negative qualities that are so obvious in the child who has received too little parental guidance.

The belief that there should be complete freedom (read license) for children is a serious mistake. Children do not have the background, knowledge and wisdom or the judgment to handle such a wide field of choice. Parents must establish limits in order to protect the child in situations that are beyond his competence and to enable the child to recognize the demands being placed on him. Otherwise he cannot learn to control himself. Learning becomes almost impossible, and the child spends much of his time testing each situation to see if any rules exist at all.

The attitude of overpermissiveness gained acceptance as a rebound from the idea of strict control, rigid schedules, and authoritarian discipline. As often happens with such reversals, the swing was exaggerated, and the children suffered from too little control. Overpermissiveness also sometimes occurs in the case of parents who were brought up strictly, never daring to act, speak, or think aggressively. They use their own children to express the unreasoned spontaneity and aggressiveness they themselves were denied, and their own psychological need blinds them to the fact that the child's behavior is offensive to others and disturbing to the child.

Firmness without domination

Parents can make definite demands firmly, since conditions are most readily accepted when it is clear that parents mean what they say. But firmness can slip into domination—forcing one's will on the child. Firmness without domination requires practice in mutual respect. Parents must respect the child's right to decide what he intends to do, and respect also their own competence by refusing to be placed at the mercy of an unruly, capricious child. They must temper their firmness with enough flexibility to make exceptions when necessary, and they must have enough humanity to admit when they are wrong. The parents' own personalities and forms of family interaction have a great deal to do with how the balance between permissiveness and firmness is worked out in everyday life. Some parents (without guilt or submissiveness) can be remarkably uncontrolling without spoiling; others (without harshness or irritability) can be quite strict and still not cramp the development of their children. There is no one way for all parents. Whichever way is used by a parent should be his way and consistently so.

Parents and punishment

Frequent misbehavior on the part of the child or failure to live up to what is expected of him by the school, the family, or parents is particularly painful for parents because of their sense of failure at their most important job. They become angry and upset at themselves as well as at their child. Often they lash out blindly without doing what is first necessary—trying to understand the problem before trying to solve it. It is more important to look into the causes of disobedience than to put faith in control by punishment alone. Are demands on the child too great? Do they fit the child, his particular personality, his age, his temperament, his sex? Are they suited to the child's needs and abilities at his particular stage of development? Is discipline clear? Is the child being forced into compliance by bullying, bribing, yelling, hitting? What are the child's feelings about his parents and others who have authority over him? [7]

Parents are increasingly aware that it is unwise to make the child ashamed of his feelings. They must of course help him control his acts by setting limits on what he does, but they should also take the child's feelings into account. This requires an individualized approach, for every child has different feelings and different reactions.

When misbehavior occurs—and it invariably does, at one time or another—it is particularly important for the parent to understand the nature of discipline. The old adage, "Spare the rod and spoil the child," belongs to the days when the only meaning of discipline was punishment and the only method of training was force and pain. Discipline does bring some conflict. But it is (or should be) a conflict aimed not just at eliciting the desired behavior, but at training in self-control.

Good discipline is a positive force directed toward what the child is allowed to do rather than what he is forbidden to do. It is based mainly on mutual love and respect. In childhood, discipline has to be reinforced with teaching, firmness, and reminder. Punishment is only one form of reminder, a particularly vigorous one for situations that warrant it.

Punishment is no longer seen as the only way to make children behave. To be sure, there will always be times when behavior calls for correction. But the most effective kind of punishment is that which follows logically from the misbehavior. Punishment is not a way of "getting even" or taking revenge, but a mode of teaching. The act at issue should bring its own consequences whenever possible. (This cannot always be the case, of course. Sometimes the act is far too dangerous, and sometimes it offers short-term gains that would reinforce the child's tendency to repeat it.)

Frequently, the child who has misbehaved knows he should be corrected and he really wants to be. Often he prefers physical discomfort or a specific penalty that he can count on in advance, so that he can weigh the pleasure of doing what he wants against the punishment he knows will follow. This helps him to see the world as consistent and reliable and is useful when he is young, but ultimately it is a less-than-successful shortcut to compliance that only seems easier than the long process of learning to be responsible for doing what he knows is right. No quick substitute has yet been found for the slow development of self-direction and self-discipline.

What the parents do is not nearly so important as how they do it. The child's interpretation of how his parents do anything to him is largely a product of how he feels about them. The child does not become obedient (though he may conform) because of the strength of a punishment; he becomes obedient in response to his desire for approval and his regret at his parents' disapproval. Parents can assist in this process by tempering the quality of their disapproval; by explaining calmly, plainly, and briefly why they disapprove; and by strengthening the positive aspects of discipline whenever possible.

All parents, even those who solemnly resolve not to, punish children at times. As we know, punishment is necessary on occasion. But as frequently as discipline is used for discipline and obedience, it just as frequently expresses impatience and anger. Even the most patient and tolerant parent can give way to anger at the culmination of a series of intensely irritating actions by the child. At such times parents may show less control of themselves than they would like the child to have. Parents are human and they can make lots of mistakes. But as long as these mistakes occur against the background of a reasonable, kind, and loving relationship with the child, and as long as parents can admit their errors and correct them quickly without holding a grudge, no irreparable damage will be done. Again, what the parent is is more important than what the parent does.

It is not, after all, the punishment itself that is important. It is the lesson the punishment was meant to teach. If a child is secure in the feeling that he is loved and wanted, that his parents care about him and have confidence in him, he will not be upset unduly by an occasional slap or other punishment. This response is to him an indication that the situation really was serious, that the parent really meant what he said. When the parent has to punish a great deal, however, it indicates a failure of discipline and an unsatisfactory relationship between parent and child. Constant spanking can induce humiliation and resentment, leaving the child resentful or intimidated, the parent chronically angry and guilty. More intense forms of corporal punishment are an indication of real disruption in the parent-child relationship and a sign that professional help is needed.

Rearing children who will become mature, self-disciplined individuals requires mature, self-disciplined adults as parents. But parents are human beings—they have moments when they are impatient, angry, or unfair with their children, when all their emotional maturity evaporates in an outburst of negative feeling. Occurring occasionally, such outbursts are not going to cause a major disturbance in the child's growth; they are a part of his learning to live with others. Occasional explosions will not harm a fundamentally good relationship.

No parent always responds to his children in an ideal way, and he should not try to hold up that kind of standard for himself. Parents are human, and children can accept human actions if they can count on the parents' basic love, understanding, and consistency. A child who feels alone, struggling against criticism and hostility, has little chance to internalize the external controls that are placed on him. But there is no end to the progress a child can make when he knows that there are adults who will help him, guide him, and allow him to go ahead because they have confidence in him.

Reciprocally, when the child reacts positively in this way, his reaction strengthens the parents' capacity for self-discipline, or allows for completion of their arrested development in this area. The parent's desire for his child to be proud of him, to love and admire him, is as strong an influence on his own behavior as is the corresponding desire of the child on the child's behavior.

Empathy and discipline

When a parent understands what is going on in himself, he can better understand what to do and how to respond to his child. There is a child in every parent who needs to learn discipline. There is a parent in every parent who needs to be capable of disciplining the child within himself. Respect the child and the parent within yourself as you would respect the child whom you are parenting. Parenting reactivates a concern with the child in you. This concern need not detract from your concern for your child, and it can be used constructively in his behalf. Empathy is a critical component between parent and child in all areas of growth and development, but it is particularly needed in the teaching and learning of self-discipline.

References

1. D. Hunt, PARENTS AND CHILDREN IN HISTORY. THE PSYCHOLOGY OF FAMILY LIFE IN EARLY MODERN FRANCE (New York: Basic Books, 1970).
2. *Ibid.*
3. H. Moller, "Childhood Before the Enlightenment" (book review), *Psychotherapy and Social Science Review* 5:16-18, 1971.
4. Karl S. Bernhardt, DISCIPLINE AND CHILD GUIDANCE (New York: McGraw-Hill Book Co., 1964).
5. E. James Lieberman, "The Disturbing Child and Family Therapy," *Clinical Proceedings of the Children's Hospital* 27:245-249, 1971.
6. Haim G. Ginott, BETWEEN PARENT AND CHILD (New York: The Macmillan Co., 1965) p 97.
7. Stella Chess, Alexander Thomas, and Herbert Birch, YOUR CHILD IS A PERSON (New York: Viking Press, 1965) p 87.

5

VARIETIES OF PARENTHOOD EXPERIENCES

Individuals marry and have children, either oblivious to the dangers involved or under the general impression that for them the joys of parenthood will predominate and they will be relatively free of its sorrows.

The joys of parenthood are experienced when a state of harmony exists between such diverse and powerful forces as the biological and emotional needs of children, the responses and expectations of parents, and the requisites and demands of society. The sorrows of parenthood are experienced when these forces are antagonistic to one another and when efforts to regain harmony are too difficult or even futile. It is apparent that with such diverse and powerful forces at work, harmony is likely to prevail less often than disharmony. Its relative infrequency may contribute to the heightened pleasure parents experience during times of genuine harmony.

On being an adoptive parent

Infertility. The following paragraphs deal with the issue of infertility and adoption, terms that have expressed the expected causal relationship in the past. The previous experience that adoptive parents were not fertile has been modified by current events. The whole adoption picture has changed radically in the last few years. Emphasis nowadays is on the so-called hard-to-place children, coupled with a critical shortage of white healthy infants (and currently nonwhite healthy infants are also in short supply). As a result, the eligibility criteria for adoptive parents have correspondingly changed and many more placements are being made than formerly with couples who have themselves given birth to children. This is an important change despite the attention to infertility given in the next few paragraphs.

By the time a marital couple has decided to adopt a child, they usually will have gone through a number of difficult and growth-inducing experiences. This decision may be reached after a couple has had to face the fact that they are not fertile and are unable to produce their own children.

To face such a fact means that one has had to change a basic expectation about oneself, yet most children take it for granted they will be fertile. So, of course, do most adults, until they find out differently. It is difficult to change an image of oneself from a person who is fertile to that of one who is not. Usually, a couple will go through a series of disappointments and stressful experiences before they finally accept the fact of infertility. The agony of waiting for pregnancies to materialize, the disappointment of not carrying them to term, and the repeated experience of sadness and loss are all part of changing the image of oneself.

There is the self-doubt that has to be faced about the function of one's own body. There are the repeated frustrations that must be endured with the failure of progressive medical procedures to result in pregnancy. Then there is the strain of sacrificing sexual intercourse as a spontaneous expression of feeling between the spouses in deference to the need for synchronizing sexual relations with the time of ovulation.

Accompanying all this is the feeling of shame or guilt about not being able to become pregnant. Usually this is felt mostly in relation to one's spouse, although one's own parents and parents-in-law may play prominent roles in this aspect of the problem. Such feelings tend to lower one's self-esteem, which is the greatest hazard of the ordeal. A husband or a wife may even blame the self or the mate for infertility and perceive it as a punishment for past sins.

Nonfertility in a couple tests the strengths of their relationship, as well as the strength of each partner individually. For each and for each other, the experiences of facing themselves as infertile are painful and injurious. Regardless of the source, men in general find these injuries harder to assimilate than do women. Often, in fact, wives feel quite protective of their husbands while both are undergoing the preliminaries that will result in the decision to adopt a child.

Ambivalence about becoming a parent. When all the medical procedures and examinations prove futile, still another self-doubt may arise: Could the nonfertility have a psychological basis? Does one really want a child? Even a physician may raise this question out of his own frustration and despair because his efforts have failed to result in pregnancy or yield a definitc reason why the infertility exists. The question is not an idle one. Natural and adoptive parents alike must face the ambivalence implicit in becoming a parent.

What this means is that it is natural for prospective parents to have second thoughts about having a child. Does one want to change the status quo? There are arguments for both sides of this question, yet most prospective parents by the end of nine months feel they want their baby, even though pregnancy may have started when both parents were not ready for it. As parents come to find out, this is not the same thing as not wanting a child—witness the parents who blame each other for failures in contraception, along with unwanted or unexpected pregnancies.

Adoptive parents go through a similar experience, but their feelings may be much more intense. In a natural pregnancy, both parents go through a series of psychological dilemmas in one way or another. Each trimester of pregnancy presents its own dilemmas. In the first trimester, many wonder what change in the relationship between them will develop with the coming of their child. Both know there will be a change, but they do not know what it will mean. In the second trimester, they begin to wonder what kinds of parents they will be. Will they be adequate to their task? How will they compare to their own parents? Will there be fun in taking care of the child? They also come to realize that there will be some frustration in raising him. One has to be able to share one's spouse with a helpless child. Can one bear the sacrifice? In the last trimester, they face the fear that "everything may not turn out all right." "Will there be something wrong with the baby?" "Will my wife come through childbirth without disaster?"

Preparation for parenthood. Facing and living with these unanswerable questions plays a significant part in the preparation for parenthood and helps the individual to make the jump from the self-image of a nonparent to that of a parent. The process of natural pregnancy is central to the experience of parenthood, because one changes one's image internally as one undergoes it. The adoptive couple, in planning for and actively seeking a child to adopt, also asks the same questions during the first and second trimesters but must await the arrival of the baby before they can understand once and for all that they are parents. Some observers believe that it takes longer to feel parenthood truly and that the adoptive mother and father must rely on the response of the baby to their care before they can feel they are truly parents.

There is a controversy in professional circles about whether the process of natural pregnancy is central to the experience of parenthood. Those who hold to a biological view of parenthood, at least in terms of emphasis, take the position that the natural parents were the real parents and that the adoptive parents can never fully feel a total sense of parenthood. Others give greater emphasis to experience and parental behavior and to parent-child relationships in the acquiring of a full sense of parenthood. The human infant, differing from the newborn animal, is least developed in instinctive responses to care for himself. This makes him the most susceptible to responses learned from the mother-infant relationship, so that the parents who care for and raise a child are infinitely more important to the child than any distress he experiences by having been deprived of his natural mother.

The real issue here is to recognize the importance of adoption agencies, whose services help mobilize the parenthood potential of the would-be parents.

What the childless, prospective adoptive parents must go through to obtain a baby gives them their own kind of preparation for parenthood. The frustrations of infertility need not be overpowering. When faced and lived with, they can call forth the psychologic strength and readiness for parenthood that the child will need. Changes in adoption practices have taken place in recent years. No longer is it necessarily a "baby" who is being adopted; many children are now being placed who are over a year old.

The adoptive couple may face a number of experiences that are not common to parents who undergo natural pregnancy. One of the more surprising to prospective adoptive parents is the difference in attitudes they encounter, as compared to those accorded natural pregnancy. Everyone seems to give support to a pregnant couple that is not forthcoming in the case of a couple seeking to adopt a child. It is as though people cannot identify as readily with adoptive parents as they can with natural parents and cannot feel the same enthusiasm for adoptive parenthood. Furthermore, once a couple has successfully adopted a child, they find themselves running into a subtle ambivalent attitude toward the adoptive experience in others whose remarks often make them feel a persistent desire to remind them of the fact of adoption. "When will you tell him he's adopted?" "How did you ever find such a good child?" "Sometimes I wish I had an adopted child along with my own children. I'd want to see if I'd raise him any differently." "Don't you ever wonder what her real parents were like?"

Such remarks convey attitudes of discrimination and prejudice, constantly emphasizing as they do the difference between adoptive and natural parents. These attitudes may infuriate some adoptive parents, especially since they may tend to deny that there is any difference between themselves and natural parents. Such denial is probably a reflection of the adoptive parents' continuing need to cope with the fact of infertility—again an indication of how painful the experience can be.

Sources of distress to adoptive parents. Another burden on the adoptive parents is their intense desire to be adequate parents. This is a drive and a goal for almost all parents, but is often more worrisome to adoptive parents. It seems to be of greater concern to adoptive mothers than to adoptive fathers, although it is obviously not restricted to adoptive parents.

Adoptive mothers sometimes feel they have a double responsibility—not only to their child but also to the mother who has given up her baby to be raised by another woman. Sometimes, too, rescue fantasies persist in adoptive mothers: "I must do a better job as a mother, be better as a parent than his own mother was to him." Or, "My child was born out of wedlock—I must do more for him than his own mother was able to do." The adoptive mother may have negative feelings about the biological mother, who has in effect rejected her child, not just been unable to care for him. Such feelings are occasionally revealed in adoptive parents' later explanations of parentage.

Some adoptive mothers are distressed to find that after the new baby enters the family, the husband does not seem as close as he was before the baby arrived. In part, this feeling is natural, since there is not too much for him to do at the time except enjoy the baby. But when his wife gives so much of herself to the new child, her husband may feel less important to his wife than before. And the appearance of the baby may become a constant reminder of his own possible infertility where its cause is unknown.

A major frustration a man bears when he and his wife are

nonfertile is that he feels robbed of the proof that he is the equal of his own father by having a child. A man usually feels gratitude to his wife, especially during the first pregnancy, because she has given him the chance to attain a new status in his life by becoming a father; that is, he can have children like his father. He can, of course, gain this satisfaction in other activities of his life, but having one's own child is often a major vehicle for the feeling that one is growing in stature and competence. As a way of dealing with the major frustration of infertility, some men do not become as involved with their adopted child as they might with their own. They may not feel fatherly toward their adopted child so much as they feel brotherly. It is surprising to physicians to find adoptive mothers who consider their husbands as one more child in the family, and not really of equal status as a parent.

Another major task in the raising of adopted children that parents of natural children do not have to perform is that of helping an adopted child accept the fact that he has had another set of parents. The problem varies in severity, depending on the age at which the child was adopted, and also the age at which he is told of his adoption.

If a child is more than two years of age when he is adopted, he will bring with him into his new family a set of images of the parenting adults around him prior to adoption. The fact that these images are already formed and that seemingly the child will not give them up can be upsetting to some adoptive parents. Such evidence that the child has had other parents may interfere with the fantasies of the adoptive parents that they are the most important persons in the child's life; or it may somehow put the child "on loan." They may not feel they have sole responsibility for him and his future. As a result, parents who adopt a child more than two years old often do not feel as close to him as they do to the child they have adopted in the first year of life.

Adoptive parents need not feel guilty about such differences in feeling because these arise from something over which they have no control, the need of the adopted child to keep his images of his natural parents Actually, the child, as he grows, learns unequivocally who his father and mother are by reason of their parenting. He makes a clear distinction between the parents who care for him and raise him and those who merely birthed him. Anxieties in the adoptive parents can be alleviated by the recognition that some of the child's difficulties in adaptation are occasioned by moving to a new home, to a new community, changes difficult for the nonadoptive child as well.

When to tell the child about adoption. There is still controversy as to when to tell a child he is adopted. For some parents, this uncertainty is upsetting, because many feelings in the adoptive parents are often activated by the need to tell the child he is adopted. Most adoptive parents, at some time or other, harbor the fantasy of not telling their child that he is adopted. The reasons for this are natural. Old hurts will be reactivated. Telling a child he is adopted reminds one of one's infertility (when this was a factor in adoption) and the pain that accompanied it.

But adoptive parents also sense that their adopted child must face a deeper distress when he has to come to grips with the fact that his natural mother gave him up. Qualified opinion seems to differ on this issue. Some psychiatrists do not believe the adopted child is necessarily distressed by losing his natural mother. Experience has shown that older parentless children —not only spontaneously, but through their adoptive parents' own conviction—can feel more that they have gained their adoptive parents than that they have lost their "real" parents, especially where they never had a normal child–parent relationship but were brought into adoption from foster homes, institutions, or painful natural-parent situations. It is a peculiar facet of the psychology of adopted children that they rarely perceive the natural father as also having failed to keep them and rear them.

Adoptive parents are naturally reluctant to have to give their child unsettling and painful news, but they come to recognize that this must be done as part of their parental responsibility, since it has to do with the child's very identity. Parents tell their child out of affection for him, but also out of respect for themselves and their child in having no secrets that could interfere with their relationship. On this basis, the thinking, planning, and execution of informing their child can be a manifestation of confidence that they have the strength and character to do it and that the child will have the strength to receive such information and cope with it.

The timing of telling a child he is adopted is based on a sense of the child's readiness for it. Compulsive repetition of the fact of adoption over a period of time, when it has no connection with the everyday life of either child or parents, makes the child suspect that adoption is a stigma and that his adoptive parents do not like him as much as they would have liked their own child. As with all important news, the child will ask questions about the facts of his adoption a number of times, unless he gets the message that he should not ask about it. A most natural time to talk about adoption is when the child asks where babies come from. He can then be told that he came from the uterus of another woman. At the same time he can be told how nice it was that he was at hand when his parents were looking for a child. They can also emphasize the fact that he behaved so pleasingly that his adoptive parents got the idea he wanted to go with them. This thought of himself as contributing in the "choosing" process gives the child some sense that he not passive victim of abandonment by his own parents, but could (and did) do something about what seemed a helpless situation. Complete honesty between parent and child will enrich the relationship and add to the dignity that accompanies such an occasion.

The stage can be set so that the adopted child may ask questions repeatedly about his natural parents and himself. The years between seven and ten are thought generally by many professional persons to be a good time to tell him about his adoption and help him adapt to the idea. However, other experienced professionals do not believe this and recommend early recognition of the adoption, when the parent is personally able and ready to talk about it. There is a right time for the parent as well as for the child, and their readiness should be interlocked on an individual basis rather than by rule of thumb.

As he approaches adolescence, the adoptive child will, in his fantasies about his natural parents, generally come to idealize and idolize them. To many adoptive parents, this may seem quite unfair to have the absent parents thought better of than are they themselves, who daily cope with the difficult tasks of raising the child. This fantasy by the adopted child is one way open to him for dealing with the lowered self-esteem inherent in the fact of abandonment. It is a phase in the integration of one's self concept which the child will have to work through again in adolescence.

Adolescence, in any family, will throw the family out of emotional balance. This is true for families with their own children and is even harder on the family with an adopted child. At some point in adolescence, the adopted child will ask again about his natural parents. The need for the child to have as much information as he can get may seem to be intense. The normal challenging and confrontation of parents by children may take on painful aspects in adoptive families. The child may use the fact of his adoption against his parents, reminding them that they are not really his parents and asking them why he has to obey them. The belittling of parents that usually takes place at some time during adolescence may be much harder for adoptive parents to take than it is for natural parents. Understandably, both adoptive parents and adopted children feel certain psychological strains that natural parents and their children do not. But clinicians do not see the larger number of adoptive families that compare very well with other selected family populations.

In late adolescence, some adopted children feel the need to search for their natural parents. They may want to travel to their birthplace in the hope of uncovering some clues relating to their origin. They may ask to see their birth certificate. Fantasies about their parents often take on romantic and unreal characteristics. All this is part of the process of clarifying their identity—a necessary growth experience. Being as honest as one can, and telling the adopted adolescent where he can get information about his origins if it exists, is often enough to satisfy him. All adolescents fantasize about their parents, some even denying that their parents are really their own, some at least questioning whether they are. The adopted adolescent deals with the fact that his natural parents are not available to him for reality testing, and his fantasies about them may persist longer. When he is eighteen years old, he can legally ask in many states to see his birth certificate. Telling him it is available but that he will have to wait is important, for making the birth certificate available is something his adoptive parents cannot do and the child is given the responsibility of finding out more about himself when he is ready to learn more.

In summary, the rearing of adopted children involves tasks shared by every parent and every child. For adoptive parents, it is the acceptance of the different experiences they must undergo and their recognition of the uniqueness of their own parental tasks as different from those of natural parents that give them the authority and confidence to find satisfaction in their roles. When the adopted child comes to have his own children, his adoptive parents may feel somewhat envious because the child is having an experience that was denied them. But their realization that the child they raised wishes to become a parent in his own right, and that this is an outcome of their adoptive parenting, is a joy of parenthood hard to surpass.

On being a step-parent

In our society, the role of step-parent is poorly defined. There is a considerable body of folklore that pictures a step-parent as a cruel and depriving person who is out to make life miserable for stepchildren. A number of popular novels and television programs have depicted the difficulties and pitfalls in the developing relationships between step-parents, natural parents, and their children. Despite great public interest, there is very little scientific writing about step-parents and the problems they encounter as members of the family.

One of the first problems a step-parent may encounter in joining a family is that of accepting any unhappy results of prior difficulties just as though he were the natural parent. However competent, mature, and artful as a parent, the step-parent may not be able to succeed completely in doing this. The reason is clear enough: a step-parent invariably has to share his role with the parent who is missing from the original family, whether by divorce or death. The step-parent may be expected to share with the absent parent such parental functions as educational planning for the children, financial support, and coordination of vacation plans and holiday visits, if the natural parent is living. If the natural parent is dead, often the step-parent may have to share ideals, moral training, and preferences for religious affiliation. The reality of the natural parent, dead or alive, is important to the step-children's development of their own identity, but it complicates the role of a step-parent.

Some students of this subject feel that a step-parent is continually exchanging the roles of parent, step-parent, and nonparent. One of the confusing aspects of his job is to know what role he should be playing and when to switch roles without resentment or self-pity. It is easy to see that in the everyday experiences of living he is a parent in terms of discipline, planning family experiences, and setting limits on the children's behavior. He is a step-parent when certain activities, visits, and planning must be shared with the absent natural parent. And he is a nonparent, when, for whatever reasons, he stands back and lets the spouse handle some aspect of the family relationship in which he does not or does not want to take part.

Some step-parents are so sensitive and aware of the "wicked stepmother" or "cruel stepfather" stereotype that they go to extremes not to take a position or attitude with their stepchildren about anything, or they minimize their involvement with them. Sometimes, too, the step-parent has to carry the burden of his spouse's oversensitivity to his reactions to his stepchildren, and the children's reactions to the step-parent as well. The natural parent may feel guilty about having separated the children from the absent parent and will not allow the step-parent any authority over them or will interfere, thus rendering the step-parent impotent in some aspects of his parental role. Another complication sometimes appears as the natural parent's fervent wish that the step-parent be a full-fledged parent and act as though he or she were the natural parent.

No step-parent can actually take the place of the natural parent in the home, but some step-parents indulge in the fantasy that they can. Or they may lay a trap for themselves by fantasying that they may be a near-perfect parent compared to the natural parent. Frequently the children will interpret such behavior as the banishment by the step-parent of the natural parent from the household and naturally they resent it. Sometimes natural parents are fearful that the new spouse may resent the extra burden of caring for the children and they may even feel guilt about imposing on the step-parent the tasks of raising children. In such circumstances it is not uncommon that the natural parent in the family keeps more control of the children than is required simply in order to relieve the step-parent of the added responsibility for the children, who, in turn, may interpret this as rejection of them on the part of the step-parent.

The ability of a step-parent to function as a parent is very much dependent on how he feels he is doing in the eyes of spouse and stepchildren. The growth of confidence in his new role is strongly influenced by the feedback of feeling and attitudes from the new family. Attitudes toward a step-parent vary with the many complex feelings in the life history of a family that accompany its transition from intact, to broken to step-parent family. If divorce was marked by anger, hostility, and blame on the part of the natural parents, this negative feeling usually persists and becomes part of the step-parent's inheritance when he joins the family. Unresolved relationships between the natural parents can interfere with the full development of the relationship between the step-parent and his spouse. From the step-parent's point of view the children may act as a reminder that the spouse has been previously married. They remain the significant tie to the old relationship. Jealousy may arise, and fear of losing control over one's relationship with one's spouse, along with the fear that there persists a relationship between the natural parents that will cloud one's own relationships.

The stepchildren themselves can interfere, in ways of which they are not fully aware, with the relationship between the step-parent and the new spouse. When one enters into marriage before any children are on the scene, there is time for husband and wife to develop their marital roles before they have to develop their roles as parents. Also, when children do arrive, there is time to develop gradually one's role as a parent during the period of pregnancy and as the children later pass through succeeding stages of growth. When a step-parent marries a spouse with children, however, there is no time to develop the functions of the marital role before he also has to develop those of a parent. Under the best of circumstances this is difficult. It becomes much more so when the natural parent and the children are still struggling with anger, hostility, and blame left over from the previous marriage.

Under such circumstances the children are likely to have intensified feelings about the step-parent. If their natural custodial parent remarries, the children are called upon to share the one parent on whom they most depend with an adult who also makes emotional demands on him. This is felt by the children as a psychological separation from the parent, and is very often an upsetting experience for them. A child, especially a young child, may be terrified by the fear that he will be abandoned by the parent he needs so much, and he looks at the step-parent as an unwanted intruder. On the other hand, a child may be so hungry for a significant relationship with a new parent that he literally demands to have him or her all to himself and may resent the time the newlyweds have to have to themselves. Some children are very confused about having two fathers or two mothers, and until they sort out in their own minds the new roles the natural parent and the step-parent assume, they are irritable, fearful, and angry. The step-parent needs to make clear early in the relationship with his stepchildren that he or she is not there to take the place of the natural parent. Some step-parents actually do have the fantasy that they will replace the child's absent parent, that they will be liked much more than the absent one. When this development fails to materialize, some step-parents withdraw and become more of a nonparent than a parental figure.

At times children feel guilty about liking a step-parent better that the natural parent who is no longer in the home. This situation frequently arises when the absent natural parent has made attempts to undermine the relationship between the step-parent and the child. In such a situation the child is apt to be more damaged than the step-parent. Sometimes nothing can be done to prevent the hostile absent parent from trying to make the child a "go-between" of the two families. The child generally handles this dilemma by tuning out the offending parent or by withdrawing somewhat from the relationship until he develops a growing understanding of the displaced parent's behavior. The step-parent can best help him by not trying to win him over or comfort him about his upset feelings. The child can be told that his parent's failure was as a spouse—the failure as a parent need not be emphasized. The child will find this out for himself later on, if he is not already beginning to sense it.

A step-parent may find the children, after a visit to their absent parent, irritable and angry. Some of the child's anger at his own parents may be displaced onto the step-parent, since he may feel safer in expressing anger toward the new parent than toward the real source. The answer for the step-parent is not to take this anger personally, when he obviously is not responsible for it. To react angrily in retaliation may only verify for the child the correctness of his behavior in the first place, and this will interfere with his full acceptance of his good feelings about his step-parent.

A more trying variation of this situation for a step-parent occurs when he marries into a family where the absent parent has died. Frequently, the dead parent comes to be overidealized by one or more of the children. Moreover, the guilt in the family members over the death of the parent may interfere with the normal process of having their grief for their dead parent gradually become less intense. To hold on to the memory of the dead parent, some children will invidiously compare their step-parent to the dead parent. The best way to cope with this situation is to be frank about the good points of the deceased, but at the same time not agree to the comparison. Avoiding defensiveness about oneself is much the best solution. If the step-parent finds he cannot help being defensive, he should consider counseling.

In some families a special problem arises between adolescent children and their step-parent. With their own parents children experience the usual barrier between daughter and father, son and mother that prevents daughters from becoming too close sexually to their fathers, and sons to their mothers. The incest taboo is a strong one in our culture. The barrier between a step-parent and children of the opposite sex is not so strong, however, and the taboo not so imperative.

The ordinary intimacy that usually exists among members of a family may at times become highly sexualized in meaning. Fondling, kissing, and hugging take on meaning beyond the usual parent-child interactions. This is more pronounced when there is a considerable discrepancy in the ages of the natural parent and the step-parent. The classic example is that of the middle-aged father with adolescent children who marries a young woman closer in age to some of the children than to her husband. The channeling and control of sexual feelings in any family is a part of the family's contribution to the future healthy sexual lives of its members. When these feelings threaten to get out of bounds, adolescent children need to be able to appeal to their natural parent for some help in the matter. If they feel this is not possible, some run away, while in other families disturbing emotional symptoms appear such as depression or hysterical complaints. All these disturbances are a cry for help and recourse to such help is indicated. Consultation with a family adviser or physician, or with one of the professional counselors available in most communities would be desirable.

Many step-parents find numerous satisfactions in their relationships in their families. Many stepchildren, too, have warm feelings toward their step-parents, and have gained immeasurably in their growth toward maturity and wisdom in ways they never would have gained without a step-parent. In this chapter, there has been sharper focus on the problems often inherent in the step-relationship, for these are the source of happiness in the family. Recognition of these problems is a beginning in working them out.

On being a parent married to a step-parent

If possible, the children should have the chance to become acquainted with their step-parent before the marriage. Such preparation and sharing of the parent-to-be allows children to become familiar with the feelings that accompany the introduction of a new family member into the family group. These feelings are generally a mixture of delight, apprehension, confusion and uncertainty as to whether they will be liked by the new parent and whether they can like him or her in return.

An important question in a young child's mind is whether he must give up one of his natural parents when he acquires a new one. The difficulty here is that the child must clarify for himself the difference between a biological parent and a parent who becomes a parent by taking care of the child and his daily requirements. The need of a child to keep in communication with his biological parent lies in the fact that so much of his basic identity is related to this person, even though this parent does not rear him.

The biological parent who remains with his or her children should make it clear that the parent who is no longer a part of the immediate family will remain important to them. If the parent outside the home is disruptive of the new family, ways must be taken to control this, for no family can live long with chaotic division of itself. But every important step in effecting control needs to be communicated to the children and in addition the reasons why such steps are necessary for their well-being.

The children of course will be getting messages from the resident parent about the new spouse and step-parent. They pick up attitudes not from words but from the nonverbal communication of facial and body expressions, of tone of voice and inflection. Trust, confidence, love, caring for, and acceptance are what is desired, with enough for the children as well as the new spouse. The children are being asked to share the parent with the step-parent, and they may experience this as a loss or as an additional source of love. Once children learn that adults have an emotional and social life apart from them but that they nevertheless will be taken care of and loved, they experience relief. Parents must assume the burden of showing the children that everyone's needs in the family can be met.

The parent faces chronic disability in his child

Illness is an unfortunate but expected experience of parenthood. However, a child's chronic illness or disability always comes as a shock. In acute illness there is strain and worry, but the experience is tempered by memories of health and growth, and recovery is expected. There is convalescence, and daily progress toward return to health. Chronic illness is a different story—a continued story with no happy ending probable.

Whether the illness or disability is recognized in infancy or at a later period, the parent goes through the same reactions: shock, disbelief, depression, anger, denial. Other diagnosis is sought. When advice is given, more often it relates to the parent's responsibility to the child. Very little is offered to help the parent himself in facing the gigantic problems he sees looming ahead. The effect of the child's condition on the parents is often overlooked. The phenomenon of parental mourning for the child who might have been is not uncommon.

There are still people who look upon the child's illness or disability as divine punishment for the sin of a parent and some who believe this often perceive the seeking of help for the child as defying God. It is the parents as well as the child who suffer, and frequently the parent suffers more than the child.

Parents often question their part in the tragedy. Are they unfit parents? Was the illness due to genetic or familial deficiency? Was prenatal care inadequate? Should another specialist be seen? Protection of the young is seen by parents and by society as a basic parental responsibility and here is a constant reminder of failure.

Acute illness raises some of these same questions, but there is dramatic action to be taken and often a sense of achievement in meeting the emergency even though fear may blot out awareness of everything except the illness. During the often trying days of convalescence, the parent can express impatience, since he knows the child's return to health is only a matter of days or weeks.

With chronic illness there is no such promise of full or rapid return to health. This often makes it difficult to conceive any hope of controlling or mitigating the chronic disability. To be told that the child must always take medication and will be limited in learning or activity imposes a heavy sentence on the parent that can lead to pity for the child and thus to overprotection.

Today, there is a general acceptance of glasses and hearing aids for very young children. But how often does a member of the family or a stranger say "poor child," and how rarely does anyone comment on this obvious evidence of parental care and planning? Doubtless people of grandparent age, who know they soon will need the same aids, tend to protect their own feelings—they forget the years of poor vision, the accusations of stupidity to which many of their own childhood peers were subjected before they were given vision or hearing tests. In general, we are just beginning to witness public acceptance of braces and prostheses as being in the same category with glasses and hearing aids. Even so it is not easy for parents to accept these disabilities in their own children.

There has long been a myth about children's cruelty to their disabled or ill peers, yet when children are left to their own devices, they play with and accept such children at their own level of functioning. They are frank in saying another child cannot hear or run. They ask the child many questions about what it "feels like." They give him roles in play that acknowledge his limitation. However, from one point of view, this is real acceptance of the child as he is. It is adults who advise children to "feel sorry for" a playmate, who wonder if his disability may not in some way be catching or at least will not be copied by other children. The overprotective and fearful parent may so often warn and intervene that both the handicapped child and his playmates come to see him as truly "different." It is not the children who will bring unhappiness to the child and his parents so much as the often well-meaning adults. Nevertheless, the parent of a handicapped child cannot escape living with and dealing with such persons and their attitudes each day.

A certain tendency to compare offspring is inherent in the parenting function—otherwise "Beautiful Baby" contests would never be held. Even when comparison is less overt, the parents of a handicapped child may often wonder why it had to be their child, may find themselves trying to will away the reality of his handicap. This is a completely understandable reaction and only causes problems when guilt at the thought results in "smother love" rather than "mother love," or when self-doubt is so great that the parents attempt to push the child far beyond his abilities. And even here the damage is doubtless due more to the child's perceiving how disappointed his parent is in him than to the actual pushing. Many a healthy but unlovely little girl or a healthy but small little boy has experienced this same devastating revelation. Each parent has a dream of what his child will be, and it takes time to realize that a child is not a dream but a person in his own right. Perhaps this is even harder for the parent of a handicapped child to realize.

Most parents adapt to the handicapped child's needs and abilities. Many have made amazingly effective plans for their disabled child and as a result have a mature, well-balanced adult son or daughter. The parents of a 13-year-old girl with paralysis after poliomyelitis were able to accept her in a wheelchair and yet give her a full life as a teenager, see her marry, have children, and run her own household, with no undertone of pity or sentimentality. Their attitude was shared by her younger siblings, her husband, and her children.

It is not easy to allow growth when infantilization of the child seems, at short range, to be less hard on him and easier for the family, and delays his venturing out of the home. Whether the basic problem is post-polio paralysis, spastic paralysis, diabetes, or retardation, the parent has to decide when the child is ready for the next step, literally and figuratively. The tendency to think "not yet" is to be expected, and sometimes this is the right answer for the child. Too often the advice given parents suggests that the so-called "age norms" are as immutable as the laws of the Medes and Persians and must be followed regardless of the child's individual needs and abilities. This attitude causes problems for all parents; for the parents of a handicapped child, even greater ones.

It would be good to be able to advise seeking professional counsel as to when a child is ready for new experiences, but many parents do not have access to such counsel. It is unfortunate that specialists are able to deal with the disease or disability and many are able to deal with the child directly, but questions from the parents' side of these problems often stir up so much emotion that they are avoided. Here, too, bland reassurance is less kind than practical examination of reality—but reassurance is easier on the giver.

Nevertheless, if at all possible, every parent of a handicapped child should have recourse to some knowledgeable person with whom he can freely discuss his personal doubts, questions, and feelings. A worry or question that is repressed can become magnified beyond its true dimensions. The ability of two parents to talk freely with each other is of immeasurable value, especially where neither has a secret sense of guilt or accusation. Even so, an outside counselor will be helpful at times.

Fortunately, there are many voluntary health associations that concentrate on particular handicaps and that offer three valuable services to the parent of a handicapped child: association with other parents having similar problems; a chance to improve services for and understanding of handicapped children in general; and an opportunity to learn of new advances in training, care, and treatment.

Associating with an organized group of parents will allow discussion of fad treatments that often victimize parents of handicapped children and can involve expenditures which penalize the whole family and jeopardize future care of the disabled child as well as of his siblings. Not all fads are the product of venal persons, but unfortunately some are. Each parent has an understandable doubt when those involved in establishment medicine disapprove of a "new" treatment, but if he can talk within a group of parents, he can obtain a clearer picture of the relation between promises and results.

Faith in any one person, professional or not, as having all the answers is too much to ask of an intelligent, conscientious parent eager to help his child. In a group of parents, with their many resources, there is some safety.

In so many chronic illnesses there are daily small, wearing responsibilities. If the treatment is uncomfortable for the child, it is more so for the parent. Times of medication, trips to doctors and clinics, special foods—all are nagging problems that can cause tension and worry. It is easy for parents to feel that they and only they can meet the child's needs, and so to build a wall around the family unit. But there are several undesirable possible results: the child has too few experiences with other caring adults and becomes fearfully dependent on his parents; the world of the parents becomes narrower and narrower so they have less to sustain themselves or to offer the child; other children in the family may be penalized by never enjoying the attentions of both parents and thus, in effect, are sacrificed to the handicapped child. Getting away for short periods is not neglectful of parental responsibilities but rather a way of renewing their spirits and developing a clearer picture of the child's abilities and needs. It also assures the older handicapped child that he is not a helpless infant who must always be dependent.

The child with a handicap is also a person with abilities to be encouraged, but the constant reminder of his limitation may cause his parents to concentrate on the negative aspects and so forget to look at the things the child can do well. In the end, pity may become the dominant factor in his relationship with his parents. In THE HANDICAPPED CHILD the authors comment as follows:

> Pity, however sincere and well-intentioned, is not good for anyone, straight or deformed, crippled or sound of limb. Because it is bestowed on those considered less fortunate or less able than the one who does the pitying, it makes the object feel inferior. It further weakens the weak, and causes those singled out to receive it for their "difference" to feel more different. As a parent, you have much better things to give your child than pity.[1]

It must be added that pity for the child may in time backlash on the parent as self-pity—a reaction that will certainly make the parent's job more difficult.

Every child gains from his parents the inner strength necessary to cope with his world. The handicapped child has a somewhat different world with which to cope, and his parents, too, have a somewhat different task in preparing him for life. For them the problem will be to establish reality-measured goals and to avoid demanding too much of themselves. They, too, are human and should allow for their own normal human feelings and reactions.

Parental reactions to loss

Bereavement in reaction to loss during parenthood has characteristics in common with bereavement during any other stage of development. At the beginning of parenthood there is the sense of loss for the previously unencumbered stage of freedom from responsibility for a child. What is commonly presented in literature and the mass media as joy and pleasure on the arrival of a new addition to the family is sometimes seen clinically as grief and even depression (postpartum depression) that can follow the new arrival, more highly publicized in the mother than in the father. The mother's depressions are easily observed and have become a part of the literature. They vary from transient to deep-seated reactions. The father tends to react to loss of the preceding stage of freedom by denial and acting out. He may get drunk or become involved in other activities that prevent his being present at the birth of the baby. Under these circumstances the mother suffers a double loss, loss of her previous state and loss of her husband at a time when she may need him desperately. The grief and depression seen in some new mothers may be caused more by the loss of the idealized image of her husband than by the loss of her pre-mother status. She tends to take her husband's abandonment as a rejection of herself without being aware that it may be more a rejection of the role of father than of husband. Of course it can be both. The activity of the husband is an example of a repetition of an historical event in his life. Such repetitions are observed in parents at these times.

The statement is made in this report that once a parent, always a parent. Yet this state of being is reflected more in attitudes than in reality. Children do grow up and go away; parents are left alone to grieve their loss and move on to the next stage. Not only is this seen in the "empty nest" syndrome as described elsewhere, but even when the child is younger. Clinically it is observed that some mothers report never having felt better than during pregnancy and during the first eight to eighteen months of the child's life. Then they may become anxious or depressed. What is lost here so early is loss of control over the infant. Once the infant asserts a personality of his own, a mind of his own, fusion ends and separation begins. The loss of a valued, idealized, needed state is recognized.

During parenthood the individual may have to cope with the fact of death—an experience restricted to this stage only (example: death of a parent or of a mate). "Bereavement states vary according to the personality of the bereaved, the relationship between the bereaved and the lost loved or valued object, and the values or institutions of the society of which the bereaved is a member." [2]

The loss that is uniquely characteristic of parenthood, however, is perhaps the most cruel and difficult loss for anyone to bear: the loss of a child. This is particularly true for the elderly, who, waiting to die, cannot understand why they were not taken instead of the child. That part of the individual which was being left for immortality disappears before he himself has died. Even in the younger parent, loss of a child is severely traumatic. The picture of a psychotic young woman denying the death of her baby by using a substitute object is well known.

Normal grief has been described in the literature:

> Normal grief includes waves of somatic distress lasting from twenty minutes to an hour: a tightness in the throat, frequent crying, sighing, a feeling of emptiness, weakness, and tension, a sense of heaviness, fatigue, lack of appetite, preoccupation with death and the deceased, a feeling of distance from other people and a loss of warmth for other people, including a tendency to respond to them with irritation and anger, handling of other people in a stiff, formal manner and much talking of the deceased.[3]

Erich Lindemann found that those who let themselves go emotionally in their grief "dealt with" it in from four to six weeks, undergoing a rapid relief of tension.[4]

Grief is a complex reaction. Crying alone does not constitute working through the loss. It is the content of emotion that matters—the necessity of letting go what no longer exists except in memories. The two opposites, hysteria and stony-faced emotional paralysis, do not represent healthy grief.

Observations of parents of a dying child disclose parental emotions of guilt, grief, and anger. These emotions will be expressed in the style of the parent's character. A parent may unremittingly and exclusively dedicate himself to care of the child. Or he may be overwhelmed by the tragedy of his child's suffering and impending death and may find it difficult to spend time with the patient who is so different from the active, healthy child he used to be.

The death of a child is experienced as unnatural, and parents feel responsibility and guilt for it. One of man's deepest fears is death before fulfillment. The parents reexperience this fear as they see the child's life ending before fulfillment. Parents have to find a meaning for the loss of a child. They fear a meaningless death.

Parenthood has been complicated today by the inability of modern man to see death as a natural part of life. Although man has a legitimate need to turn his face away from death, elaborate camouflage and rejection of the notion of death prevail in the United States. This leads to falsification of the essence of man. At the same time, the body-count from our unending wars and the killings on our highways and in the streets have made death a daily part of our symbolism.

The terror comes not only from our fear of individual death but also from our sense that nothing can be permanent. It is natural that a prominent mode or sense of immortality is derived by parents from their children, through whom they participate in the whole of humanity. Today, unfortunately, man's destructive capacity through nuclear weapons threatens this sense of biosocial immortality.

It is difficult for one to ponder death without resources, be they transcendental, inspirational, or existential. If one accepts death as inevitable rather than seeing it as unnatural and accidental, there may be less of a need to project fear of death outside oneself. This might possibly mute some of the violence of our times. Energies now used up in attempts to repress the concept of death would be available for more constructive aspects of living. In other words, rejection of the idea of death destroys a person, but acceptance may save him.

In coming to terms with their own feelings about death, parents will not only contribute to their own maturity and understanding of life but help their children by not shutting them out from the reality of death. Increased psychological compatibility with the idea of oncoming death seems called for—in our cultural upbringing generally, and specifically in the interactions within the home. In this area, books may help parents complete their own growth and, in turn, the growth of their children.[5]

When parents separate: another loss experience

Divorce, death, or a job requiring long absence from the family are the major causes of separation in a family. There are factors common to all these experiences that are of the utmost importance to the continued well-being of everyone involved.

Perhaps the most important is the way the parents felt about each other before the separation occurred. Unresolved feelings resulting in loss of love, in anger, and in loss of self-esteem can plague both parents and children if they are ignored and some attempt is not made to resolve them. Here again the parent is faced with a changing image of himself. Situations are continually occurring in life that involve a change in one's self-image.

The fact that parents are parted by reason of divorce or death does not necessarily mean that they have separated psychologically. Feelings of anger, remorse, guilt, retaliation, and sorrow for oneself, and mixtures of both hatred and love, can keep an emotional relationship going long after parents have in fact ceased to live with each other. Specifically, feelings of being hurt or of wanting to hurt the other may unconsciously persist. Inability to get the absent spouse out of one's thoughts may provide further evidence that psychological separation has not yet taken place.

How does one accomplish psychological separation? There are two processes by which this may be achieved: by working through the experience of grief or mourning or by facing and resolving one's true feelings about oneself. Both of these psychologic processes take time and both are in some degree painful. Friends, parents, and relatives who can give true emotional support during this period are most valuable. In their affection and concern, they cannot prevent one's suffering or interfere with it, but they can help one handle it. Where such persons are not available, an understanding authority figure such as a minister or family physician may help. Or someone may be consulted from the professionals most skilled in helping people to separate psychologically, psychiatrists, psychologists, and social workers.

An important reason for recognizing that one's own feelings as a separated spouse have to be coped with first is that the children going through their own separation experiences will seek help from their parents in resolving their feelings. Despite the fact that from the child's standpoint one parent can rear him and meet his physical needs, he needs two parents for his complete psychological growth and development. In order to conceptualize himself as a developing person, he must identify himself with two parents—a man and a woman, a father and a mother. If he has been exposed to only one parent in his day-to-day living, he will inevitably invent the other in his mind. To do this he will ask many questions of the parent available to him about his other parent. He will try in many ways to get some feeling, some information about his absent parent, and if this is not forthcoming, he will then in his fantasy create the parent he needs in order to feel good about himself as a person.

Of course, if parents have not resolved their own feelings about each other, this process in their children will reawaken old angers, regrets, longings, and whatever else remains. Children especially want to know how the parents actually did feel about each other when they married, for what they are really trying to find out is how both parents felt about having them.

Was the child wanted by both parents? Did both parents like him? How did they feel about his being a boy (or a girl)?

And very important, has he done anything to contribute to the separation?

Children need some positive information about both parents and their parents' attitudes toward them and each other. For purposes of building their own sense of self and their own self-respect, they need to know the assets and good qualities of their parents, as well as the liabilities and weaknesses that led to their parents' failure. They want to know what attracted the parents to each other, what each liked in the other. And although their larger understanding of why their parents separated will only come as they grow older, children need to know why their parents were divorced, why they were incompatible, and, in the case of death, why their parent died.

The child also gets the message when one or both parents indicate either by silence or by direct statement that they do not care to talk about the matter. This may make the child seek information elsewhere or adjust to the delay in obtaining it, but he cannot really drop the subject, because it involves an unresolved problem about himself that impedes the process of growth.

As they grow older, children come to realize that their parents were not perfect and in their humanity made errors and mistakes. What a child finds very hard to forgive is the derogation and demeaning of each parent by the other, or of one parent by the other. The child cannot help but feel great anger at the offending parent, for it is really degrading to the child and involves a loss of his own self-esteem. In addition, children tend to become confused about themselves in such a situation because they find it all the harder to separate those assets and characteristics that belong to their parents from those that belong to them.

Consider the nine-year-old boy whose divorced father is living away from home. He sees his father fairly regularly and likes many things about him. If he feels his mother has strong feelings of rejection for his father, has only negative feelings about him, he may have difficulty in identifying with his father. As a boy, he needs to like his father in some ways, and even be like him in some ways, but if he feels that his mother totally rejects his father, he may begin to feel that she cannot really accept him either. Since he likes his mother and is dependent upon her for affection and acceptance, he finds himself in conflict about his loyalties.

A major problem for many single parents living with their children is loneliness. Except for the children, the parent feels isolated from others. Especially when the parent also has a job, he can come to feel trapped, caught in the position of having no time for himself. In such a situation, children frequently go to a day-care center after school or during the day. When the parent returns from work to take them home and care for them at night, they often seem more demanding and emotionally draining of him than he can tolerate. Fatigue and sometimes a feeling of helplessness may intensify the distress and loneliness of the custodial single parent.

When one feels trapped and caught, with no life for oneself, this is the time to take a look at one's situation, to see what can be modified in the circumstances and what in oneself may be contributing to the crisis. Aside from the harsh reality of having to work and to raise children alone, attitudes toward himself may lock the individual in to such a trait. The parent's self-esteem may have been so damaged by his previous experiences that relating only to the children may offer protection against intimacy with other adults. Anger and resentment at the other parent coupled with failure to do anything about his problem will surely result in further feelings of isolation and deprivation.

Children need to feel that their parents have a life apart from them. They do not want to feel that the whole burden of their parents' happiness or unhappiness is on their shoulders. Furthermore, when their parents do have a life beyond that of their children, the children are able sooner to gain a clearer understanding of their own separateness and to distinguish which feelings come from themselves and which from their parents. Emotional growth is much easier and smoother.

Becoming a single parent after one has been a partner in marriage means many changes in one's social living. Going without a partner to social affairs where one's friends are paired off is for many an uneasy social experience. One's social and marital difference seems to be constantly on display. Women especially feel that social forces are pushing them in the direction of associating mainly with adults of their own sex. The sense of being a successful woman is sometimes blunted and certainly not enhanced by such feelings.

The need for social contacts is reflected in the new groups and services being offered in large cities. Computerized dating services seem to have become a permanent part of the urban scene. Single men and women have formed social groups, some of them organized by the members themselves, many as a church-sponsored social function. Therapy and educational groups composed of single parents may often be found through agencies serving broken families. Opportunities for social and educational activities are becoming more generally available. If you find you really want them but cannot seek them out, this is a sign that you have a serious conflict about yourself, and some counseling or therapy would seem indicated.

In our changing society there remain many unanswered questions about the single parent. But single parents are rapidly becoming a common and more fully accepted social phenomenon. Several organizations, like Parents Without Partners and Solo Parents, are contributing heavily in this area of education and problem-solving. They offer programs dealing with personal needs, family problems, and legal and financial matters.

Divorced persons may experience treatment as second-class citizens and the children of divorced parents may be discriminated against by their peers. Many newly divorced persons feel like failures because of the divorce and it is important for them to rebuild an adequate sense of self-esteem. Alienated temporarily from the rest of society, they go through a kind of identity crisis all over again. In such a situation they must learn to come to grips with the idea that their marital failure does not make them complete failures as human beings. As these experiences become more common in society, appropriate community education can promote in the community at large greater acceptance and understanding of the single parent and the problems peculiar to his position.

References

1. Edith M. Stern and E. Castendyck, THE HANDICAPPED CHILD (New York: A. A. Wyn, 1950) p 18.
2. B. Schoenberg et al (eds), LOSS AND GRIEF: PSYCHOLOGICAL MANAGEMENT IN MEDICAL PRACTICE (New York: Columbia University Press, 1970) p 35.
3. E. James Lieberman, "War and the Family: The Psychology of Antigrief," *Modern Medicine,* April 19, 1971, pp 179-183, 91.
4. E. Lindemann, "Symptomatology and Management of Acute Grief," *American Journal of Psychiatry* 101:141, 1944.
5. Earl A. Grollman, TALKING ABOUT DEATH (Boston: Beacon Press, 1970); Earl A. Grollman (ed), EXPLAINING DEATH TO CHILDREN (Boston: Beacon Press, 1967).

6

THE MIDDLE YEARS OF PARENTHOOD

The "middle generation"

The years between youth and approaching old age ranging between the ages of thirty and fifty-five have been termed "the middle generation."[1] In 1970 the men and women in this age group comprised about 20 per cent of the population of the United States. They are caught in the complications of a fast-changing world, the confusing mores and attitudes of their children, and the responsibilities of caring for and coping with (parenting) their own elderly parents. While they are discharging their responsibilities at home, they are carrying on their work, which comprises the major portion of the work of their society. They do not remain fixed and unchanging but exhibit the changing dynamic patterns of adulthood. They continue to grow and develop, and to adapt to their environment. During this period, the search for the meaning of life begins.

Like the middle child caught between younger and older siblings, the members of the middle generation are caught between the younger and older generations. Not only must they handle the problems of their own children, but many must care for their own parents, who may no longer be able to take care of themselves and may have regressed to their second childhood. Or their own parents may still be active parents who reserve the right to direct and criticize their grown children just as they did so many years before. Between these two extremes are parents who present to their children of the middle generation their own unique problems and dilemmas. The resulting relationships can stimulate change, as indicated in the pungent one-liner, "I never knew I had parents until I became one." Reconciliation and closeness with one's parents becomes possible as they are seen from the broader perspective of one's own parenthood.

Growth of the "middle years" parent

The experience of parenting allows the adult to appreciate the pains and sorrows that his own parents endured and enhances his capacity for empathy. Sharing the joys experienced from the new generation brings the two parenting generations closer together.

Or the natural enmity between generations may be clarified, as in the case of the young father who was watching his daughter and his severely authoritarian father playing together. The two were obviously delighted with one another and deeply enjoying the experience. The grandfather openly showed love, affection, and adoration for his grandchild. In amazement the girl's father asked his father: "Why didn't you ever play with me this way?" to which the older man replied with great tenderness in his voice, "Fool, don't you realize she and I have an enemy in common?"

Rewards of the parenting experience

The simultaneous ambivalence toward one's children and one's parents as well as simultaneous responsibility for them has positive effects. It develops the all-important capacity for empathic responses along with the characteristics of maturity as seen in wisdom, integrity, and the ability to relate on different levels to one's late-adolescent and young-adult children. The pleasures thus experienced are the pleasures of functioning well, the pleasures of pulling together the resources gained in several decades of living. This experience serves as a preparation for grandparenthood.

Main characteristic of involvement

Benedek notes that although variations among the individual experiences of the middle phase of parenthood may be innumerable, the overriding characteristic is the parents' involvement in the preoccupation with their children's sexual life.[2] Parents are intent on protecting their children, their daughters more than their sons, against the dangers of sexuality. However, even this traditional preoccupation of parents seems to be lessening in the face of the helplessness they often feel today. The current sexual revolution, touched off by the effectiveness of the pill and the increasing ease of obtaining legal abortion, has often overwhelmed parents with the sense of their own responsibility. Mothers have traditionally been more concerned and preoccupied than fathers, and their worries rarely cease until the child is safely married.

Responsibility after marriage of the child

The immediate responsibility of the parent for a child is discontinued with the latter's marriage. Legally, the child's new mate has become his next of kin. The sudden change, though often a hoped-for relief, is not easily made emotionally. Difficulties in giving up parental responsibilities are often satirized in mother-in-law jokes. For women, separation from their child seems more difficult than for men. This is particularly true for the mother who has no other involvements and whose husband is at the peak of involvement in his work.

New developmental task for parents

At the time of the marriage of a child the parents have a new developmental task.[3] They have to accept the new son-in-law or daughter-in-law, not only into the family but into their hearts as an object of their love. When a prior need is being fulfilled, this works out beautifully. There is the mother who welcomes a new son-in-law with open arms. He epitomizes the son she never had or what her own sons never became. Likewise fathers are seen who adore the son's wife. The newcomer may enhance the feelings of self-esteem and pride of the spouse's parents.

In other parents-in-law, ambivalence flares up because of concern about the happiness of their own child. The fault is too often seen in the other child rather than in their own. The developmental task for the parent then becomes one of separating from the married child and objectifying the parental relationship, thus enjoying a broader perspective and consequent lessening of ambivalence.

The empty nest

Characteristic of the problems of this period is "the empty nest syndrome." A recent survey of men and women reaching the "empty nest" period showed little evidence of attitudes of crisis.[4] The group was primarily Anglo-American, with higher blue-collar and clerical occupations the most common. Fewer than one in five reported frustrations in their new family situation. The men's frustrations were usually connected with work or money, but they, like the women, were prideful of their marriage, children, and family. The satisfactions of parenthood continued for both sexes, the empty nest notwithstanding. The prospect of an empty nest seemed not to threaten the parents of this group. Rather, they looked forward to a somewhat less complex life style with relief. Viewed in context of the past and the anticipated future, this period of diminishing parental responsibilities appeared to be favorable for both men and women.

Some families never really empty the nest. There may always be children at home, there may be grandchildren. Or the couple may have a late child, become foster parents later on, or adopt children. In other families, however, one by one the children separate from the home. Gradually the nuclear family is reduced to the parents. The nest is emptied.

In most cases, the active phase of parenthood does not end with a big bang, a final startling flash. It fades slowly, like the dimming of the houselights in a theater. Whether dimming proceeds to total darkness or the curtain lifts on a new and brighter scene depends on how husband and wife have weathered the storms of parenthood, how they have grown, and how they take up their roles in the new drama.

By the time the children are ready to leave home, parents are not the same people they were two decades before. They have changed physically, for they are approaching or are in middle age, and they have changed psychologically—hopefully toward maturity and wisdom. Some of their ways of interacting and coping with the outside world have strengthened, some have fallen into disuse, and some have developed over the years. Their social roles have changed—they are no longer the young couple starting a family and career. And society itself has changed. The explosion of knowledge and technology that occurred while they were raising their children has been accompanied by a social revolution that questions old values and has altered patterns of work and family living while creating a culture substantially different from the one they grew up in.

Different crises make people respond in different ways. When the crisis is challenging yet something one feels confident about coping with, it can be a means of growth. The crises that occur in middle age may afford just such a challenge, or they may be crises more difficult to cope with. The children leave home. Business reversals occur. The expected promotion goes to someone else. A close friend or relative dies. Serious illness is diagnosed. For the first time, after the children leave and the husband retires a couple may be together all the time. This can prove a major strain or a source of great relief and joy.

It may be the process of aging itself that precipitates the crisis. Each year the telephone book is printed in smaller type, theater and airplane seats are not as comfortably wide as they were advertised to be, stairs are getting steeper, a midweek party becomes more of an endurance contest than a celebration. The single strand of gray has broadened into streaks. Sagging jowls and double chin seem to have appeared overnight. The body as a whole has less rebound. Minor illnesses last longer, new aches and pains appear with nagging regularity.

The feelings of helplessness and uselessness that can be set off by all these developments are common enough to be recognized as a specific illness—a middle-life depression, also known as climacteric depression or involutional melancholia. It affects women more frequently than men, because women are more seriously affected by loss of the children from the home, the day-to-day care of their children has been an important part of their lives, and their emotional investment is heavier. Often the children are leaving home at about the same time the mother has to deal with the physical and emotional stresses of menopause. But men are by no means unaffected. More often, however, these stresses are experienced as minor and fleeting inconveniences by the parents, who feel in the prime of their lives. For most people, these are extremely productive and creative years.

Resolution of sexual problems

One particular problem in this age group is the resolution of anxiety concerning sex. Marital partners may find it especially difficult to work out their changing sexuality where their relationship has not been based on mutual trust, understanding, and tolerance. Women are generally more keenly aware of their changing physiology because they can observe the cessation of their menstrual cycle and the hormonal changes in their bodies. Men are more often likely to develop a "now or never" attitude about sex. They try to bolster up their self-image by means of an extramarital liaison with a younger partner or to prove their sexual prowess with a number of different partners, or they may experiment with previously untried forms of sexual expression.

Job pressures for men

In addition to his changing image as a father and a husband, the man of middle age has problems that revolve around his job. What used to be a stimulating test of his ability to succeed becomes a perfunctory routine protecting him from failure. The innovative aggressiveness that marked his early working years has given way to a "don't make waves" attitude, a preference for the tried and true methods that worked for him as he climbed the ladder. He is not sure he can keep on top of what is happening in the organization, not sure he can learn the new skills and techniques necessitated by technological change. He begins to think seriously about the company or the union pension plan. How far can he get in the company before his retirement is enforced? The higher he can push his earnings before retirement, the better his pension will be. He tries to sell himself to his superiors, while hesitating to take risks that might prove his worth over that of the innovative but less experienced younger men who threaten him.

Time for inventory

For both husband and wife, the middle years are often a time of taking inventory, assessing what they have accomplished and what resources they have with which to face the future. But this process raises questions that can be very upsetting: "If I had done it differently twenty years ago, where would I be now?" The wife remembers that she rejected the proposal of the man who is now president of her husband's company. The husband thinks of his ambition to found his own accounting firm and looks regretfully at his position as assistant bookkeeper in one of the company's branch offices.

At this time, major financial demands may be made. Husband

and wife, worried as they are about building a nest egg for their own later years, are faced with added burdens from their children. Paying for a college education, helping to launch a career, lending financial assistance when children get married, are all financial drains. Especially parents who have high aspirations for their children find that their help is needed when graduate training must be completed or a new family started.

Psychological aspects

But probably the deepest strains on the parents of middle age are psychological. When a child leaves home—to further his education, to serve in the Armed Forces, to assume a job in a distant place, or to get married—it is a loss that leaves a definite empty place in the family circle. This is not the first time that parents have felt the wrench of separation. They went through it when the child first began to assert his independence, when he started school, when he reached puberty. But now it repeats itself in a more final, less reversible way, and it rekindles the conflicts that so many parents experience about relinquishing their authority and control. Once more they have to "spiral around" and work out past conflicts and hopes. But now they have to do it knowing that the children are no longer in the home and that there is little chance to correct mistakes of the past.

Every stage of life is an opportunity to broaden and expand, or a threat causing restriction and retreat. Each stage adds new experiences and knowledge—knowledge of one's capabilities and assets, experience in overcoming one's limitations and liabilities, and increasing awareness of what life has to offer. Middle age, particularly, can bring a wealth of contentment and satisfaction. The zealous pressure of youth to challenge, change, and rebel has been tempered by a growing ability to see life as it is, to keep things in perspective. The grueling race for a mate and a career has been run, children no longer demand care round the clock, social life is no longer cut short by the caprices of babysitters or the unpredictability of childhood diseases.

There is time now for enjoyment. And because there is more time the parents whose children are grown are free to develop new talents and interests that will not only satisfy their own desire for self-expression, but will expand the reservoir of what they have to offer the society in which they live. They are able to relinquish many of their former responsibilities to the family, and so find themselves ready to assume responsibility for their own generation.

References

1. Rose N. Franzblau, THE MIDDLE GENERATION (New York: Holt, Rinehart, Winston, 1971).
2. James E. Anthony and T. Benedek (eds), PARENTHOOD: ITS PSYCHOLOGY AND PSYCHOPATHOLOGY (New York: Little, Brown & Co., 1970).
3. *Ibid.*
4. M. F. Lowenthal and D. Chiribog, "Transition to the Empty Nest," *Archives of General Psychiatry* 26:8-14, 1972.

7

GRANDPARENTHOOD

A new lease on life

If the psychology of parenthood has been a much-neglected field of study, grandparenthood has been practically ignored. Prior to Benedek's published work, the few references in the literature concerned similarities in grandchildren's gestures and attitudes to those of their grandparents. In writing about parenthood during the life cycle, Benedek chronologically places the gratifying experiences of grandparenthood as coming before the last phase of parenthood.[1] She points out that the emotional significance of grandparenthood has often been referred to as a new lease on life.

In the grandparents' search for a meaning to life, the grandchildren represent their tie to eternity—a part of them that continues in the stream of life after they have gone. If the grandparent has not established a full life of his own and has an unfulfilled need to be needed, grandchildren are a blessing. Children have an inexhaustible supply of needs—more than enough to go around for all the adults in their environment. Grandparents offer to grandchildren the advantages of the extended family and in so doing take some pressure off the nuclear family of father, mother, children.

Grandparents relive memories of their own parenthood

It is important to understand that during this period of growth and change, grandparents relive the memory of the early phase of their own parenthood while observing the growth and development of their grandchildren. Here an opportunity arises for development of the understanding, empathy, integration, and wisdom that come only with age. Even in later years change can occur. Opinions formerly prevailing that no changes occur during adulthood are being corrected by experiences with older adults, who respond surprisingly well to interest on the part of others and to opportunities for change. Of course, some grandparents, in trying to make up for failures with their own children, become less understanding, less responsible, and too indulgent with their grandchildren, and some who fail their children also fail their grandchildren.

Our original position that parents need separation from their children and freedom from dependency on their children also holds for grandparents. In American society, with its sociological peculiarities of population mobility, extended families are diminishing in number. Segregation of the elderly occurs as they become infirm. In this situation emotional self-reliance is especially important.

Not the same for everyone

It is difficult to generalize about the emotional content of grandparenthood because of several variables involved. There are differences, depending on the personalities of the individuals interacting among the three generations involved and on the cultural and socioeconomic changes in family structure.[2] Change is what is to be expected, anticipated, and accepted by grandparents. When they can accept change, the wisdom and calmness of age are attained. When they cannot, the rigidity and irritability in aging are exposed. Parenthood and grandparenthood are stages calling for continuous growth and development. Grandparenthood demands a continuing involvement in the stream of life. It delays that withdrawal of interest onto oneself characteristic of emotional preparation for death.

When grandchildren grow up

This involvement with life's activities, while furthered by grandchildren, should not center on them. Grandchildren grow up and away from grandparents. They may have time enough or be kind enough to be loving, or they may be experienced as balm for the wounds inflicted by old age. But grandparenthood is not a static state of being. Even in grandparenthood, continuing change involving separation and individuation is the order of the day.

The extended family

Various influences play a part in the development of the child. Among these, the family in which the child develops to maturity is of primary importance. Great emphasis has been placed on parent-child relationships, yet others also make a significant contribution, and certainly one of the most important of these relationships is that of the grandparents to the child. In attempting to formulate and understand the influence of grandparents, it seems helpful to think of the family as a dynamic system, a system into which new members are introduced; existent members are in a constant state of change within themselves and in relation to each other; various members drop out of the system at various times when they go away to college or get married or move out to live on their own. At times, what appears to be a dropping out may be more accurately described as a change in the relationship of the dropout to the system, while death of a member of the family system is an actual physical dropping out. The influence in a family of grandparents on their grandchildren, then, is viewed not as a one-to-one relationship but as a dynamic interrelationship within a dynamic system.

The influence of grandparents

It is clear that the influence of grandparents varies greatly from family to family and from culture to culture. Generally speaking, it can be said that the influence of grandparents on children is exerted in two important ways: first, through direct contact of varying intensity; second, through the symbolic meaning of grandparents in the family system. It is possible for a grandparent to exert a potent influence over a child even though the child has never related to him personally. In many family systems there exists a person or persons reaching beyond the second and third generations, who even as a memory exerts an influence by what he has meant to various members of the family system, thus remaining a strong and potent force in the lives of the various family members.

The most obvious and easily discernible influence exerted by the grandparent is that where grandchild and grandparent have direct contact. Parents and grandparents may live in the same house, may actually be part of the same household; or a considerable physical distance may separate the two households, with relatively infrequent physical contact. The actual degree of physical contact does not seem to be the most significant factor in the influence exerted by grandparents but rather the relative position the grandparents occupy in the total family system.

An important psychological mechanism useful to the individual is that of identification in family relationships. It is important for us all to have an awareness of our origins, and grandparents are usually the members of the family system who represent the most remote living expression of a child's origin. Grandparents can convey a feeling about his origins to a child that parents cannot convey. The fact that the grandchild is also the visible and tangible expression of the grandparent's continuance adds an important ingredient to the relationship. The grandchild is important to the grandparent in a manner somewhat different from the way in which he is important to the parents. The parent is usually investing of himself in many different areas, while the grandparents are in a varying state of divestment from many distracting activities. Putting it another way, the grandparent has more time. With grandchildren, also, grandparents seem to sense a "second chance," tend to make up for the failures they may have experienced in the rearing of their own children. This promotes greater understanding and forbearance.

Of course, these are mixed blessings. Where grandparents live in the same household with their children and grandchildren, confusion and rivalry may develop. In some instances, the grandparent becomes the parent, while the actual parent is relegated to the position of the child's older sibling, as it were. Furthermore, the parent is at a disadvantage because his feelings for the child are still ambivalent. The grandparent, on the other hand, has already exhausted his hostility and other adverse feelings on his own children so that little of it is left for the grandchild. This is why the grandchild sometimes seems to be the recipient only of the grandparent's indulgence.

Grandfather as replacement figure

The interest, admiration, and fantasies that gather round the figure of the grandfather may derive from attitudes experienced earlier in respect to the father, with some important differences. In the first place, they nearly always refer back to the earliest period of childhood. More particularly, at the time when the boy is beginning to weave his "family romance" and is engaged in "getting rid of" his real father by replacing him in his imagination with a more satisfactory figure (whence in the second great period of repression—puberty—the idea of God usually arises), the grandfather may present himself as an acceptable substitute. The replacement figure is always endowed with the qualities of the father, so that an analysis of the fantasy brings us straight back to the father himself. The grandfather is therefore peculiarly suited to play substitute because of his resemblance and relationship to the father (in the case of the grandfather on the paternal side). The process is often furthered by the greater tenderness and forbearance that as a rule mark the attitude of an older man toward children. Many a stern father becomes an indulgent grandfather in later life, in part, perhaps, because his feeling of responsibility in the rearing of children has been dulled by the philosophy of age. As the child grows older, the association already established is strengthened by the increasing resemblance of the father to the memory picture of the grandfather.

The value of the family system

In broad terms, what is required during the maturation process is the movement of a child from total helplessness at birth to relative independence at maturity. The family system provides the child with the opportunity for experiencing, in the interaction of the various members of the system, what lies ahead for him as an individual. In the grandparent can be seen the product of one member who is at the distant end of the spectrum; through him the child can establish his origins. He can see the ascendency of the parents simultaneously with the decline and possible loss of the grandparents. Within the extended family system he has the opportunity to grapple with varieties of life experiences ranging from birth, marriage, and success to death and failure, and with all the accompanying emotions. Grandparents contribute significantly to this total experience.

References

1. James E. Anthony and T. Benedek (eds), PARENTHOOD: ITS PSYCHOLOGY AND PSYCHOPATHOLOGY (New York: Little, Brown & Co., 1970).
2. *Ibid.*

8

PARENTS ARE PEOPLE TOO

"The first half of our life is ruined by our parents; the second half by our children."

"I asked my friend how his son was. He started to cry. I have stopped asking my friends how their children are."

These two quotations are painfully pertinent to our current American culture. The first is a pungent witticism that brings a smile to the reader's face; the second, perhaps, brings a tear —especially if the reader is a parent of adolescent or school-age children in today's society.

The importance of rearing children

The current generation of parents in America is often maligned not only by the younger generations but also, in their own confusion, by the parents themselves. This same generation has on occasion devoted many of its resources to the development of the young. It has been the guardian of the twentieth century tradition expressed in the question: What more important thing can you do in this world than rear healthy children?

Obviously, from other points of view there are more important activities than the rearing of healthy children. To many, a Shakespearean sonnet, a Picasso painting, a Michelangelo sculpture is a creative act far surpassing the garden-variety creativity of the rearing of children.

The importance of the nuclear family

The extended family has been the mainstay of every civilization. In America, the later phenomenon of the nuclear family—stripped of the helping hands of grandparents, aunts, uncles, and other relatives—has assumed this burden. The nuclear family is much more a definitive fact of life today than it has been in times past or in other cultures. Various forms of the extended family in an organized sense are likely to remain in the minority, albeit more visible and possibly more acceptable in family patterns of the future.

On the basic assumption that the nuclear family will continue to be the dominant family pattern, then it is clear that parents in the nuclear family must become aware of the importance of extended family functions as developed and shaped in society (schools, churches, other community resources). Parents could benefit from an education through which they might learn how to make these extensions truly functional and responsive to the needs of both children and parents.

Placing blame on parents

In contrast to such help from the culture is the hindrance of making parents feel guilty and anxious in their role. This pressure from the larger society impedes the personal growth of parents during the parental stage of their life cycle and contributes little to the welfare of their children.

For years, argument has raged between the relative importance of heredity versus environment as the cause of emotional illnesses in children. In fact, any single cause would seem unlikely. Yet emotionally inspired volumes by respected and dedicated scientists have produced heated debate over causes and cures. Frequently, this has led to attribution of blame. "And even some of the most 'objective' investigators have accepted an organizing point of view prematurely and too inflexibly. The very impulse that invigorates scientific interest may have simultaneously tended to becloud and befuddle." [1] This approach popularized such terms as "schizophrenogenic," "overprotective," "rejecting mother"—terms now becoming obsolete. The outlook presented was dangerous and one-sided.

Helping troubled people is constructive; fault-finding is destructive and short-sighted. In the field of early childhood psychoses, there is growing evidence of perceptual and neurobiological involvement, and recent studies of family characteristics tend to rule out parental psychopathology as a causative factor.[2] What has been needed here is greater knowledge, not criticism of parents.

In this monograph, we have stressed the intergenerational phenomena. The family is the psychological field in which transactional processes take place. The interest of parents and grandparents in the children brings about changes in the adults. The parents' behavior is dependent upon their past experiences, their reactions to the presence of the child, and their expectations of the future. They face continuous adaptation to physiological and psychological changes in the child, and an inner push for development is a constant force. Parents do not always have the inner resources needed to cope with the difficulties of rearing children. They may need help from other nurturing, helping adults in order to nurture the child effectively. They may find it necessary to count on the assistance of extended-family members or community resources during critical stages of the parenting process.

What this book is about

Throughout these pages we have stressed nurturing and growing oneself during parenthood and even grandparenthood. In so doing, the individual becomes more adequate as a parent, as a grandparent, and as an individual when circumstance separates him from the family, leaving him on his own. It is during this time that the hard-earned wisdom and love of humanity beyond the circle of one's family, characteristic of maturity, serve the individual well.

Changing styles of family living and parenthood

Obviously, emphasis on the importance of parenthood is a culturally conservative force. And it is from this force that every socicty, from aboriginal man onward, has structured some form of family life in which to rear, socialize, and protect the children. Opposed to this force, considerable resistance is developing, as seen in the anticultural, deeply individualistic movements in modern society. From this opposing viewpoint, the individual is more real, more fundamental than an abstraction such as "the family life style." Communal types of living free the individual from direct responsibility for the child.

Differing values seem to lie at the core of the differences between the two viewpoints. It is consistent with the desire to be a parent to believe that it is more creative to rear and shape the personality of a fine, live child than it is to work in an office or even to carve a statue. It is further consistent with the role of the parent to believe that when economic necessity does not compel it, even the best day-care center is a poor substitute for the constant one-to-one relationship of an adequate mother to her child within the setting of a nuclear or an extended family. It is also consistent that the parent, in addition to being a parent, is an individual in his own right.

Do the two views have in common the goal of developing a healthy, mature self while differing in approach? Does not the one through parenthood, and the other through activities removed from parenthood, envision the same outcome? The experience of parenthood is not essential for the successful growth and development of an individual to maturity. The experience of parenthood, *per se,* does not achieve the goal of emotional maturity. Parenthood may not be utilized positively, may even prove a deterrent, in some individuals, to self-government. Though the extended family and the nuclear family have been the mainstay of every civilization, the alternative of the commune may be utilized by people with such special needs. The successful society of the future is likely to be one that is capable of tolerating many life styles without too many abrasive interactions.

Parenthood and continuing growth

A capacity to respect individual differences and needs is consistent with the training and work of the psychiatrist. His capacity for empathy allows for equal respect for the child as a person and for the parent as a person. Both are persons progressing through their own stages of growth and development who meet at various points in time. After centuries in which children were considered to be chattels, with few rights of their own, a swing of the pendulum of public opinion took place in the twentieth century wherein their rights were vociferously championed. In the process parents were designated as the villains. The current state of confusion, anxiety, and guilt among parents about their role may give way to a period of thought and reflection forcing consideration of a change in priorities. Parents are not only vehicles for the care of their children. They were persons before the arrival of children, are persons while they are parents, and will be persons after the children leave. Parents are people, too! Their "old-fashioned" values of love and family are worthwhile. The past is not entirely "dumb." Parents should respect their own values and live by them. They were told to listen to their parents. They are now told to listen to their children. Both directives are valuable. They must, in addition, listen to themselves. Their children's lives may or may not turn out well. Too many other factors are involved to allow predictions based on what parents alone do with their children. If parents do listen and do modify their own conduct accordingly, things may not turn out as well as desired, but their own fulfillment will be solidly insured by their own growth and development.

References

1. J. N. Hingtgen and C. O. Bryson, "Recent Developments in the Study of Early Childhood Psychoses," *Schizophrenia Bulletin* No. 5, Spring 1972, pp 8-54. National Institute of Mental Health, Rockville, Maryland.
2. *Ibid.*

FOR FURTHER READING

Abraham, Karl. "Some Remarks on the Role of Grandparents in the Psychology of Neuroses," in his CLINICAL PAPERS AND ESSAYS ON PSYCHOANALYSIS (New York: Basic Books, 1955) Volume 2, pp 44-47.

Anthony, E. James. " 'It Hurts Me More Than It Hurts You' —An Approach to Discipline as a Two-Way Process," in FROM LEARNING FOR LOVE TO LOVE OF LEARNING, Rudolf Ekstein & Rocco L. Motto, Eds (New York: Brunner/Mazel, 1969) Chapter 11, pp 117-131.

Barnard, J. REMARRIAGE, A STUDY OF MARRIAGE (New York: Dryden Press, 1956).

Baruch, Dorothy W. NEW WAYS IN DISCIPLINE (New York: McGraw Hill Book Co., 1949).

Bettelheim, Bruno. "The Problem of Generations," in YOUTH: CHANGE AND CHALLENGE, Erik H. Erikson, Ed (New York: Basic Books, 1961) pp 64-92.

Bowlby, John. ATTACHMENT AND LOSS (New York: Basic Books, 1969) Volume I, Chapter 1.

Bradley, T. AN EXPLORATION OF CASEWORKERS' PERCEPTIONS OF ADOPTIVE APPLICANTS (New York: Child Welfare League of America, 1967).

Bruch, Hilde. DON'T BE AFRAID OF YOUR CHILD (New York: Farrar, Straus & Young, 1952).

Caldwell, Bettye M. What Is Optimal Learning Environment for the Young Child? *American Journal of Orthopsychiatry* 37:8-21, 1968.

Cann, H. M. & Cavallis, L. L. Effects of Grandparents and Parental Age, Birth Order and Geographic Variation on Sex Ratio, Live-Born and Still-Born Infants, *American Journal of Human Genetics* 20:381-391, 1968.

Cornwall, Georgia. Scapegoating, *American Journal of Nursing* 67:1862-1867, 1967.

Curlee, J. Alcoholism and the Empty Nest, *Bulletin of the Menninger Clinic* 33:165-171, 1969.

Deykins, E. Y.; Jacobson, S.; Klerman, G.; & Solomon, M. The Empty Nest: Psychosocial Aspects of Conflict between Depressed Women and Their Grown Children, *American Journal of Psychiatry* 122:1422-1426, 1966.

Epstein, Nathan B. "Grandparents and Parents of Emotionally Healthy Adolescents," in SCIENCE AND PSYCHOANALYSIS, Jules H. Masserman, Ed (New York: Grune & Stratton) Volume 3, pp 181-188, 1960.

THE EXCEPTIONAL PARENT (Boston: Psychological Educational Corp., 264 Beacon Street 02116).

Faegre, M. L. The Cruel Stepmother, *Ladies Home Journal* 52:72-74, Feb. 1935.

Fast, I. & Cain, C. C. The Stepparent Role: Potential for Disturbances in Family Functioning, *American Journal of Orthopsychiatry* 36:485-491, 1966.

Ferenczi, Sandor. "The Grandfather Complex," in FURTHER CONTRIBUTIONS TO THE THEORY AND TECHNIQUE OF PSYCHOANALYSIS (New York: Basic Books, 1952) pp 323-324.

Gardner, Richard A. THE BOYS' AND GIRLS' BOOK ABOUT DIVORCE (New York: Science House, 1970).

———. The Guilt Reaction of Parents and Children with Severe Physical Disease, *American Journal of Psychiatry* 126:636-644, 1969.

"Generation in the Middle," in BLUE PRINT FOR HEALTH (Chicago: Blue Cross Association, 1970) Volume 23, No. 1.

Giloran, J. L. Family Happiness, *Royal Society of Health Journal* 85:211-217, 1965.

Gruenberg, Sidonie M., Ed. THE NEW ENCYCLOPEDIA OF CHILD CARE AND GUIDANCE (Garden City, N.Y.: Doubleday & Co., 1968).

Hamovitch, Maurice B. THE PARENT AND THE FATALLY ILL CHILD (Denver: City of Hope Medical Center, 1964).

Hobbs, Daniel F. Parenthood as a Crisis—A Third Study, *Marriage and the Family* 27:367-372, 1965.

Holt, Hubert (M.D.) & Winich, Charles (Ph.D.). Some Psychiatric Dynamics in Divorce and Separation, *Mental Hygiene* 49:443-452, 1965.

Jones, Ernest. "The Significance of the Grandfather for the Fate of the Individual," in his PAPERS ON PSYCHOANALYSIS, 4th ed (London: Bailliere, 1938) pp 519-524.

Johnson, G. P. Delinquent Boys, Their Parents and Grandparents, *Acta Psychiatrica Scandinavica* Vol 43, suppl. 195, 1967.

Kahana, B. Grandparents from Perspective of Developing Grandchild, *Gerontologist* 8:31, 1968.

Kalish, R. A. Of Children and Grandfathers: A Speculative Essay on Dependency, *Gerontologist* 7:65-69, 1967.

Kanner, Leo. IN DEFENSE OF MOTHERS (Springfield, Ill.: Charles C Thomas, 1951).

Keniston, Kenneth. YOUNG RADICALS (New York: Harcourt, Brace & World, 1968).

Kirk, H. D. SHARED FATE (New York: Free Press of Glencoe, 1964).

Lidz, Theodore. "The Person," in MARITAL CHOICE (New York: Basic Books, 1968) Chapter 13, pp 386-410.

Lindemann, Erich. "Problems Related to Grandparents," in UNDERSTANDING YOUR PATIENT, S. Liebman, Ed (Philadelphia: J. B. Lippincott, 1957) pp 147-158.

Longoer, Thomas S. Broken Homes and Mental Disorder, *Public Health Reports* 78:921-926, 1963.

Loomis, W. G. Use of a Foster Grandmother in Psychotherapy of a Preschool Child on a Pediatric Ward, *Clinical Pediatrics* 6:384-386, 1967.

Malinowski, Bronislaw. "Parenthood the Basis of Social Structure," in THE NEW GENERATION: THE INTIMATE PROBLEMS OF MODERN PARENTS AND CHILDREN, V. W. Calverton, Ed (New York: Macauley Co., 1930).

Mendelson, R. S. & Gold, J. G. A Foster Grandchild Program, *Pediatrics* 41:691, 1968.

Meriam, A. S. THE STEPFATHER IN THE FAMILY (Chicago: University of Chicago Press, 1940).

Meyerowitz, J. H. & Feldman, Harold. Transition to Parenthood, *Psychiatric Research Reports* (American Psychiatric Association) 20:78-84, 1966.

McDermott, John T., Jr. Parental Divorce in Early Childhood, *American Journal of Psychiatry* 124:1424-1432, 1968.

Neubauer, Peter R. One Parent and His Oedipal Development, *The Psychoanalytic Study of the Child* 15:286-309, 1960.

Pederson, F. A. & Sullivan, E. J. Relationships among Geographical Mobility, Parental Attitudes and Emotional Disturbances in Children, *American Journal of Orthopsychiatry* 34:575-580, 1964.

Rappaport, Ernest A. A Grandparent Syndrome, *Psychoanalytic Quarterly* 27:518-538, 1958.

Rasmussen, Margaret, Ed. DISCIPLINE, International Bulletin 99 (Washington, D. C.: Association for Childhood Education, 1956).

Robin, A. J. Motivation for Parenthood, *Journal of Projective Techniques* 29:406-413, 1966.

Rogers, Peter. Influence of Losing One's Parent on Being a Parent, *Psychiatric Digest* 29:29-36, 1968.

Rybak, W. S. Psychosocial Changes in Personality during Foster Grandparents Program, *Journal of the American Gerontological Society* 16:956-959, 1968.

Schecter, M. D. Observations on Adopted Children, *Archives of General Psychiatry* 3:21-32, 1960.

Schecter, M. D.; Carlson, P. V.; Simmons, J. Q.; & Work, H. H. Emotional Problems of the Adoptee, *Archives of General Psychiatry* 10:109-118, 1964.

THE SINGLE PARENT (Washington, D. C.: Parents Without Partners, Inc., 7910 Woodmont Avenue 20014).

Smith, W. C. THE STEPCHILD (Chicago: University of Chicago Press, 1953).

Snell, John E., Rusewald, Richard J. & Robey, Ames. The Wifebeater's Wife, *Archives of General Psychiatry* 11:107-112, 1964.

Solow, Robert A. Psychological Aspects of Muscular Dystrophy, *Exceptional Children* 32:99-163, 1965.

Stern, Edith M. & Castendyck, Elsa. CARE OF THE HANDICAPPED CHILD (New York: A. A. Wyn, 1950).

Van der Veen, F., Heubner, B. & Jorgens, B. Relationships between the Parents' Concept of the Family and Family Adjustment, *American Journal of Orthopsychiatry* 34:45-55, 1964.

ACKNOWLEDGMENTS TO CONTRIBUTORS

The program of the Group for the Advancement of Psychiatry, a nonprofit, tax-exempt organization, is made possible largely through the voluntary contributions and efforts of its members. For their financial assistance during the past fiscal year, in helping it to fulfill its aims, GAP is grateful to the following:

Sponsors

CIBA Pharmaceutical Company
The Commonwealth Fund
The Division Fund
Maurice Falk Medical Fund
The Finkelstein Foundation
Geigy Pharmaceuticals
The Grant Foundation
The Grove Foundation
The Holzheimer Fund
Ittleson Family Foundation
The Olin Foundation
Reader's Digest Foundation
A. H. Robins Company
Roche Laboratories
Sandoz Pharmaceuticals
Schering Corporation
Mrs. Sylvia Schwartz
The Murray L. Silberstein Fund
The Lucille Ellis Simon Foundation
The Norton Simon Foundation
The Smart Family Foundation
Smith Kline & French Laboratories
van Ameringen Foundation, Inc.
Lawrence Weinberg
Wyeth Laboratories

Donors

Virginia & Nathan Bederman Foundation
Harper & Row, Publishers
Orrin Stine
The Stone Foundation, Inc.

PUBLICATIONS OF THE GROUP FOR THE ADVANCEMENT OF PSYCHIATRY

Because readers of this publication may not be aware of previously published GAP titles, a selected listing is given below:

NO.	TITLE	PRICE
38	The Diagnostic Process in Child Psychiatry—Aug. 1957	$ .75
56	Mental Retardation: A Family Crisis—The Therapeutic Role of the Physician—Dec. 1963	.50
60	Sex and the College Student—Nov. 1965	1.50
62	Psychopathological Disorders in Childhood: Theoretical Considerations and a Proposed Classification—June 1966	4.00
68	Normal Adolescence: Its Dynamics and Impact—Feb. 1968	1.50
78	The Field of Family Therapy—March 1970	3.00
80	Drug Misuse: A Psychiatric View of a Modern Dilemma—June 1970	1.00
82	Crisis in Child Mental Health: A Critical Assessment—Feb. 1972	2.00

Orders amounting to less than $5.00 must be accompanied by remittance. All prices are subject to change without notice.

GAP publications may be ordered on a subscription basis. The current subscription cycle comprising the Volume 8 Series covers the period from July 1, 1971 to June 30, 1974. The subscription fee is $15.00 U.S.A. and $16.00 Canadian and other foreign, payable in U.S. currency.

Bound volumes of GAP publications issued since 1947 are also available. They include GAP titles no longer in print that are unavailable in any other form.

Please send your order and remittance to: Publications Office, Group for the Advancement of Psychiatry, 419 Park Avenue South, New York, New York 10016.

This publication was produced for the Group for the Advancement of Psychiatry by the Mental Health Materials Center, Inc., New York.